READINGS ON

FLANNERY O'CONNOR

OTHER TITLES IN THE GREENHAVEN PRESS LITERARY COMPANION SERIES:

AMERICAN AUTHORS

Maya Angelou
Stephen Crane
Emily Dickinson
William Faulkner
F. Scott Fitzgerald
Robert Frost
Nathaniel Hawthorne
Ernest Hemingway
Arthur Miller
Eugene O'Neill
Edgar Allan Poe
John Steinbeck
Mark Twain
Walt Whitman
Thornton Wilder

AMERICAN LITERATURE

The Adventures of
  Huckleberry Finn
The Adventures of Tom
  Sawyer
Black Boy
The Call of the Wild
The Catcher in the Rye
The Crucible
Death of a Salesman
Ethan Frome
Fahrenheit 451
A Farewell to Arms
The Glass Menagerie
The Grapes of Wrath
The Great Gatsby
Of Mice and Men
My Antonia
Native Son
The Old Man and the Sea
One Flew Over the Cuckoo's
  Nest
Our Town
The Pearl
A Raisin in the Sun
The Red Pony
The Scarlet Letter
A Separate Peace
To Kill a Mockingbird
Twelve Angry Men

THE GREENHAVEN PRESS

Literary Companion

TO AMERICAN AUTHORS

FLANNERY O'CONNOR

Jennifer A. Hurley, *Book Editor*

David L. Bender, *Publisher*

Bruno Leone, *Executive Editor*

Bonnie Szumski, *Series Editor*

Greenhaven Press, Inc., San Diego, CA

Library of Congress Cataloging-in-Publication Data

Readings on Flannery O'Connor /
    Jennifer A. Hurley, book editor.
        p. cm.
    Includes bibliographical references (p.) and index.
    ISBN 0-7377-0561-2 (pbk. : alk. paper) —
ISBN 0-7377-0562-0 (lib. bdg. : alk. paper)
    1. O'Connor, Flannery—Criticism and interpretation.
2. Women and literature—Southern States—History—
20th century. I. Hurley, Jennifer A., 1973–

PS3565.C57 Z847 2001
813'.54—dc21

                                                00-049480

Cover photo: Flannery O'Connor Collection,
Ina Dillard Russell Library, Georgia College and
State University, Milledgeville, Georgia
Library of Congress, 17

Copyright © 2001 by Greenhaven Press, Inc.
PO Box 289009
San Diego, CA 92198-9009
Printed in the U.S.A.

Where the artist is still trusted, he will not be looked to for assurance.

—Flannery O'Connor,
Mystery and Manners

CONTENTS

other prominent writers of the American South; however, she differed from her fellow Southerners in that her vision of the world was fundamentally religious.

Chapter 2: O'Connor's Predominant Themes

Chapter 3: A Critical Selection

her position in society are challenged when she is attacked in a doctor's waiting room by a surly college student.

FOREWORD

*"'Tis the good reader that
makes the good book."*

Ralph Waldo Emerson

The story's bare facts are simple: The captain, an old and scarred seafarer, walks with a peg leg made of whale ivory. He relentlessly drives his crew to hunt the world's oceans for the great white whale that crippled him. After a long search, the ship encounters the whale and a fierce battle ensues. Finally the captain drives his harpoon into the whale, but the harpoon line catches the captain about the neck and drags him to his death.

A simple story, a straightforward plot—yet, since the 1851 publication of Herman Melville's *Moby-Dick*, readers and critics have found many meanings in the struggle between Captain Ahab and the whale. To some, the novel is a cautionary tale that depicts how Ahab's obsession with revenge leads to his insanity and death. Others believe that the whale represents the unknowable secrets of the universe and that Ahab is a tragic hero who dares to challenge fate by attempting to discover this knowledge. Perhaps Melville intended Ahab as a criticism of Americans' tendency to become involved in well-intentioned but irrational causes. Or did Melville model Ahab after himself, letting his fictional character express his anger at what he perceived as a cruel and distant god?

Although literary critics disagree over the meaning of *Moby-Dick*, readers do not need to choose one particular interpretation in order to gain an understanding of Melville's novel. Instead, by examining various analyses, they can gain numerous insights into the issues that lie under the surface of the basic plot. Studying the writings of literary critics can also aid readers in making their own assessments of *Moby-Dick* and other literary works and in developing analytical thinking skills.

The Greenhaven Literary Companion Series was created with these goals in mind. Designed for young adults, this unique anthology series provides an engaging and comprehensive introduction to literary analysis and criticism. The essays included in the Literary Companion Series are chosen for their accessibility to a young adult audience and are expertly edited in consideration of both the reading and comprehension levels of this audience. In addition, each essay is introduced by a concise summation that presents the contributing writer's main themes and insights. Every anthology in the Literary Companion Series contains a varied selection of critical essays that cover a wide time span and express diverse views. Wherever possible, primary sources are represented through excerpts from authors' notebooks, letters, and journals and through contemporary criticism.

Each title in the Literary Companion Series pays careful consideration to the historical context of the particular author or literary work. In-depth biographies and detailed chronologies reveal important aspects of authors' lives and emphasize the historical events and social milieu that influenced their writings. To facilitate further research, every anthology includes primary and secondary source bibliographies of articles and/or books selected for their suitability for young adults. These engaging features make the Greenhaven Literary Companion series ideal for introducing students to literary analysis in the classroom or as a library resource for young adults researching the world's great authors and literature.

Exceptional in its focus on young adults, the Greenhaven Literary Companion Series strives to present literary criticism in a compelling and accessible format. Every title in the series is intended to spark readers' interest in leading American and world authors, to help them broaden their understanding of literature, and to encourage them to formulate their own analyses of the literary works that they read. It is the editors' hope that young adult readers will find these anthologies to be true companions in their study of literature.

INTRODUCTION

First-time readers of Flannery O'Connor may experience a wide range of reactions to her stories—including shock, amusement, disgust, or simply bewilderment—but very few are apt to be bored. Like no other writer, O'Connor knows how to capture her readers' attention. The world, as she depicts it, is a bizarre but fascinating place, full of killers, lunatics, idiots, cripples, and even hermaphrodites. In the realm of O'Connor, a woman's face is "as broad and innocent as a cabbage"; a valise is said to resemble "the head of a hippopotamus." Even nature seems peculiar, sometimes menacing: Her similes turn the sun into a "furious white blister" or "a huge red ball like an elevated Host drenched in blood," and a cloud into a "turnip."

O'Connor has a sense of the mysterious equal to that of any horror writer—as a young girl, she admired the tales of Edgar Allan Poe—but she is also astoundingly funny. One writer stated about "A Good Man Is Hard to Find" that although five people get murdered in the story, "you'd have to call it a comedy." O'Connor's particular blend of the tragic and comic makes her readers laugh while shuddering at their own laughter.

Because her fiction has the power to astonish even today's audiences, to whom violent images have become almost commonplace, readers are sometimes surprised to learn that O'Connor, a devout Catholic, regarded her stories as Christian. Her primary interest as a writer was to show her characters experiencing a moment of grace—defined in Christian orthodoxy as God's act of unmerited love toward man—that helps them find redemption. The outrageous violence that occurs so frequently in her work is, as O'Connor once stated, "strangely capable of returning my characters to reality and preparing them for their moment of grace."

Although O'Connor intended her stories to be read as Christian parables, her fiction is enjoyed by readers of all religious faiths—and of none. Her work continues to intrigue scholars and students because of its rich insight into human nature. As Tony Magistrale, professor of English at the University of Vermont, writes

> O'Connor's stories are about people struggling with one another, trying to wrest victories from the recalcitrance of love and fate. They are about the triumph and failure of will, the divine and the human, and about the tragic consequences of our own flawed perceptivity, which quietly stalk us all, like age and death. In spite of the brutal fates that so often befall her characters, O'Connor possesses a genuine sympathy for them. . . . This sympathy is born from a common humanity, the awareness on O'Connor's part that all of us share in concert the fundamental condition of sin and the possibility for spiritual advancement once we recognize the devil's hand within our own.

Students who read O'Connor will undoubtedly take pleasure in her hilarious cast of characters; hers are some of the most memorable characters in literature. Those who take the time to study O'Connor's themes will experience a deeper satisfaction. The essays in *Readings on Flannery O'Connor*, excerpted from the best critical examinations of her work, are intended to enhance students' understanding of and appreciation for O'Connor's strange and wonderful fiction.

FLANNERY O'CONNOR: A BIOGRAPHY

Flannery O'Connor never cared much for literary biographies. In a talk she gave to a group of English teachers, she warned against the danger of allowing biographical information to overshadow an author's work. "A work of art exists without its author from the moment the words are on paper," she stated, "and the more complete the work, the less important it is who wrote it or why. If you're studying literature, the intentions of the writer have to be found in the work itself, and not in his life."

In O'Connor's own case, scholars have often made faulty assumptions about her life based on her stories. Some critics, noting the similarities between O'Connor's life and the lives of her sour intellectuals—such as Hulga in "Good Country People" or Julian in "Everything That Rises Must Converge"—have concluded that she was lonely, miserable, and pessimistic. However, as the following biography will show, O'Connor was neither friendless nor unhappy; in fact, one of her most visible traits was the joy she took in life—especially Southern life, which she loved for its eccentricities.

EARLY LIFE

Mary Flannery O'Connor, the only child of Catholic parents Edward Francis and Regina Cline O'Connor, was born in Savannah, Georgia, on March 25, 1925. She spent her childhood there, attending the parochial schools of St. Vincent's Grammar School and Sacred Heart, until 1938, when the family moved to Milledgeville, Georgia, where Mrs. O'Connor's father had been mayor for several years. That same year, Mr. O'Connor was diagnosed with disseminated lupus, an incurable disease of the immune system.

As a student at Peabody High School in Milledgeville, thirteen-year-old Mary Flannery had already developed a diverse set of interests: She rode horseback, designed lapel pins that she sold at a local store, and raised a tame goose and a quail named Amelia Earhart. She also wrote and illustrated three books about geese, *Mistaken Identity, Elmo,* and *Gertrude,* which she was unable to publish. Her first published works—cartoons—appeared in the *Peabody Palladium,* the student newspaper at her high school.

In February 1941, when she was just shy of sixteen, her father died of lupus. The following year, Mary Flannery graduated from high school and enrolled in Georgia State College for Women (GSCW), also in Milledgeville. She majored in social science—a field that she would later disparage in her letters and fiction. She also served as the editor of the newspaper, feature editor of the yearbook, and editor of the literary quarterly *The Corinthian.* Although she wrote stories for *The Corinthian,* Mary Flannery considered herself a cartoonist, not a writer. During her years at college, her humorous cartoons depicting life on campus appeared in almost every publication the college produced. She created most of her cartoons by linoleum block-printing—a process by which a design is etched or cut into a sheet of linoleum, ink is applied to the linoleum, and the image is printed onto a piece of paper.

AT THE WRITER'S WORKSHOP IN IOWA

Mary Flannery's dream at that time was to publish her cartoons in the *New Yorker.* The magazine had rejected her work, but encouraged her to make further submissions. However, she was unexpectedly granted a place in the University of Iowa's prestigious Writer's Workshop on the basis of her short stories, which had been submitted by one of her English teachers at GSCW. She accepted the offer and made plans to move to Iowa.

Feeling that her two first names would be an anomaly in the Midwest and not wanting to be known as Mary O'Connor, she officially dropped "Mary" from her name. Still, her Southern heritage did not go unnoticed. Paul Engle, director of the Writer's Workshop, reports that during his first meeting with O'Connor in 1946, her native Georgian accent was so thick that he could not understand a word she was saying. He recalls that "embarrassed, I asked her to write down what she had just said on a pad. She wrote: 'My name is Flannery O'Connor. I am not a journalist. Can I come to the Writer's Workshop?'"

Engle describes the stories O'Connor wrote for his class as "quietly filled with insight, shrewd about human weaknesses, hard and compassionate." He remarks that she was shy about having her stories read aloud, and

> when it was her turn to have a story presented in the Workshop, I would read it aloud anonymously. . . . Flannery always had a flexible and objective view of her own writing, constantly revising, and in every case improving. The will to be a writer was adamant; nothing could resist it, not even her own sensibility about her own work. Cut, alter, try it again. . . . Sitting at the back of the room, silent, Flannery was more of a presence than the exuberant talkers who serenade every writing-class with their loudness. The only communicating gesture she would make was an occasional amused and shy smile at something absurd. The dreary chair she sat in glowed.

O'Connor's ambition to be a published writer was realized relatively early. In 1946, her first year at Iowa, *Accent* magazine published her story "The Geranium." Shortly after her June 1947 graduation with a Master of Fine Arts in Literature, she sold "The Train" to the *Sewanee Review*, and "The Capture" to *Mademoiselle* magazine. Furthermore, based on excerpts from her first novel, *Wise Blood*, the Rinehart publishing company awarded her $750—a sum that would serve as an advance on royalties if the company ultimately accepted the novel. Intending to finish the novel for publication by Rinehart, O'Connor requested a position as a guest writer at Yaddo, an artist retreat in Sarasota Springs, New York, and was offered an invitation in 1948. She lived there from June 1948 until February 1949, when a controversy erupted over a guest who was accused of being a Communist spy. At Yaddo, O'Connor was known for her ascetic existence; she rarely took part in the festivities held by the other guest writers. Poet Robert Lowell, who also lived at the retreat, teased O'Connor for many years about a party she attended, during which she slipped going up some stairs and broke her bottle of gin before drinking any.

A RESOLUTE YOUNG WRITER

Although O'Connor was a young writer—she was only twenty-three when she began working on her first novel—she knew what her goals were and could not be persuaded to change them. This is most clearly illustrated by her reaction to Rinehart editor John Selby's criticism of *Wise Blood*, given during the period that O'Connor lived at Yaddo. After reviewing nine chapters of the novel-in-progress, Selby wrote O'Connor saying that he thought she was a "straight shooter" and a talented writer, but that her book suffered from a "peculiar aloneness." Upon receiving these comments, O'Connor immediately wrote to her agent, Elizabeth McKee:

> Please tell me what is under that Sears Roebuck Straight Shooter approach. I presume . . . either that Rinehart will not take the novel as it will be if left to my fiendish care (it will be essentially as it is), or that Rinehart would like to rescue it at this point and train it into a conventional novel. . . . I feel the objections they raise are connected with its virtues, and the thought of working with them specifically to correct these lacks they mention is repulsive to me. The letter is addressed to a slightly dim-witted Camp Fire Girl, and I cannot look with composure on getting a lifetime of others like them.

However, in an effort to honor her commitment to the Rinehart publishing agency, she wrote to John Selby the following day, stating that

> I can only hope that in the finished novel the direction will be clearer . . . I feel that whatever virtues the novel may have are very much connected with the limitations you mention. I am not writing a conventional novel, and I think that the quality of the novel I write will derive precisely from the peculiarity or aloneness, if you will, of the experience I write from. . . . In short, I am amenable to criticism but only within the sphere of what I am trying to do; I will not be persuaded to do otherwise. The finished book, though I hope less angular, will be just as odd if not odder than the nine chapters you have now.

Selby, convinced that O'Connor was "prematurely arrogant" about her talents, eventually released her from her contract, leaving her free to consider other interested publishers. O'Connor signed a contract to publish *Wise Blood* with Robert Giroux, then an editor at Harcourt, Brace and Company. She worked on the novel while living briefly in a one-room apartment in New York City, and then in Ridgefield, Connecticut, at the home of fellow Catholic writers Sally and Robert Fitzgerald, who became two of her closest friends.

AN ATTACK OF LUPUS

In December 1950, when the Fitzgeralds put O'Connor on a train to Georgia for a visit home, she was feeling slightly sick; by the time she arrived at the train station several hours later, she looked, as her uncle later said, "like a shriveled old woman." Soon afterwards, she was diagnosed with lupus, the same disease that had taken her father's life. She spent the next nine months desperately ill in an Atlanta hospital, where doctors believed that she was dying. Fortunately, blood transfusions and injections of a cortisone derivative, ACTH, pulled her through the worst of the illness, and she was finally released from the hospital in the summer of 1951.

Because O'Connor could no longer climb the stairs of her mother's home in Milledgeville, Mrs. O'Connor moved to a family farm five miles from town. "Andalusia," as O'Connor named the farm, would be their permanent home. She and

Due to lupus, an incurable disease that weakens the immune system, O'Connor depended on crutches for much of her adult life.

her mother established a daily routine at Andalusia: In the mornings, O'Connor wrote for three hours—a period of time that she considered inviolable—then the two traveled to town for a formal lunch at the antebellum house owned by O'Connor's aunt. In the afternoons, she tended to her birds. Since the age of five, when she had owned a chicken that walked backwards, she had collected various types of fowl. Her interest grew into a passion; over time, she acquired a small zoo, consisting of more than forty peahens and peacocks, over a dozen Chinese geese, ducks that she had smuggled home on a plane from Connecticut, and a scruffy pair of swans. In an essay that appeared in *Holiday* magazine in 1961, she writes that when she uncrated her first flock of peafowl, she said, "I want so many of them that every time I go out the door, four or five run into me." An amateur oil painter, O'Connor often painted pictures of her fowl. She often sent a photograph of one of these, a self-portrait with a peacock in the background, to people who requested a picture of her.

During her first year at Andalusia, O'Connor's general health continued to improve, but the daily shots of ACTH, which she administered herself and described as "scarcely less disagreeable than the disease," weakened the bones of her hips, so that by 1955 she would be forced to use crutches. The disease, or perhaps the medicine, also affected her appearance—a fact that she bore without bitterness. Robert Giroux, her editor at Harcourt, writes that

> Flannery had less vanity than anyone I had ever known. When I asked her for a photograph to use on the book jacket [of *Wise Blood*], I expected a picture taken before her illness. The new one she sent was not unattractive, and she looked out at the reader with that clear-eyed gaze of hers, but her hair had not fully grown back nor had the puffiness induced by cortisone wholly subsided.

An Emerging Talent

In 1952, *Wise Blood*, the novel she had been writing and rewriting for the past six years, was finally published. The reviews praised her abilities as a writer, but found her novel confusing and strange; as Giroux put it, the reviewers "all recognized her power but missed her point."

O'Connor was not overly concerned with the mixed reviews of *Wise Blood*—she was busy at work on a collection of short stories. Most critics agree that it was at this time that her talents truly began to flourish; over the next three years, she seemed to write one masterpiece after the other, including "A Good Man Is Hard to Find," "The Life You Save May Be Your Own," "The Displaced Person," "The Artificial Nigger," and "Good Country People." Catherine Carver, an editor at Harcourt, brought each of these stories into Giroux's office with the comment, "Wait till you read this one!" In 1955, ten of her short stories were published as a collection entitled *A Good Man Is Hard to Find and Other Stories*—a collection that received high praise and confirmed O'Connor's status as a great contemporary writer. British novelist Evelyn Waugh wrote about the advance proofs sent to him: "If these stories are in fact the work of a young lady, they are indeed remarkable." However, O'Connor was frustrated by reviews that called the stories, with their incidents of shocking violence, "brutal and sarcastic." In her opinion, the stories were

> hard but they are hard because there is nothing harder or less sentimental than Christian realism. I believe that there are many rough beasts now slouching toward Bethlehem to be born and that I have reported the progress of a few of them, and when I see these stories described as horror stories I am always amused because the reviewer always has hold of the wrong horror.

Catholicism was not simply O'Connor's religion; it was the meaning of her life and the reason why she wrote. As she wrote in an essay entitled "The Fiction Writer and His Country,"

> I see from the standpoint of Christian orthodoxy. This means that for me the meaning of life is centered in our Redemption by Christ and that what I see in the world I see in its relation to that. . . . I have heard it said that belief in Christian dogma is a hindrance to the writer, but I myself have found nothing further from the truth. Actually, it forces the storyteller to observe.

O'Connor's devout Catholicism is not always evident to those reading her stories; the Catholic Church rarely appears in her work at all, and her religious themes elude some readers. It is her letters to Betty Hester, a friend sometimes known by pseudonym "A.," that gives the clearest picture of her faith. Betty Hester first wrote O'Connor in 1955 to express her appreciation of *A Good Man Is Hard to Find*. Pleased with Hester's astute observations about the stories,

O'Connor responded with a long letter. Thus began their written correspondence, in which the two traded books and periodicals, shared amusing tidbits from their day-to-day life, and exchanged views on a wide range of subjects: religious faith, the Catholic press, literature, philosophy, and social and political issues. Hester eventually became a regular visitor at Andalusia and in 1956, O'Connor acted as the sponsor for her friend's confirmation as a Catholic. She was devastated when Hester decided to leave the Church five years later; however, their friendship continued much as before.

In fact, contrary to popular views of O'Connor as a hermit, she had a number of friends who visited her at the farm and with whom she kept up a close correspondence. O'Connor was an avid letter-writer; it was not uncommon for her to send several long letters every day. From her letters, one gets a sense of her hospitality toward friends and strangers, her passion for her work, her sense of humor—sometimes scathing and sometimes silly—and her fascination with the absurd details of life. Sally Fitzgerald writes that

> the world of the absurd delighted her. She regaled us with Hadacol advertisements; birth announcements of infants with names that had to be read to be believed; such news items as the attendance of Roy Rogers' horse at a church service in California. . . . All these things filled her with glee, and gleefully she passed them on. She could write fine country talk, of course, and often did, to amuse her friends and herself. The next letter, however, might set forth in strong clear style a literary or theological insight that shed light in every direction.

O'Connor's penchant for letter-writing led one commentator to remark that "any crank could write to her and get an answer." It is true that she responded to almost every letter that crossed her desk: compliments from people who loved her work, complaints from readers who were frustrated by her "depressing" stories, and questions from English teachers whose students were reading her stories. She even wrote back to the man who said that he hadn't read her book, but objected to her statement that "a good man is hard to find."

She welcomed the opportunity to meet her readers in person, often extending warm invitations to strangers to visit her at the farm. She was also happy to speak to local organizations and clubs, many of which held luncheons in her honor. From 1955 to 1960, when she was working on her second novel, *The Violent Bear It Away,* O'Connor accepted every speaking engagement she could manage. Her talks were intelligent, funny, and delivered in her typical deadpan style, but she did not delight in giving formal lectures. Her principal purpose in lecturing was to earn money to buy conveniences for her mother, such as a telephone and a new refrigerator that "spits ice cubes." She took pleasure in buying gifts for her mother; the two had a close relationship, and O'Connor once told a friend that her greatest fear was that she would outlive her mother.

PILGRIMAGE TO EUROPE

In the summer of 1958, O'Connor and her mother traveled to Europe—the first time out of the country for both of them—with a group of Catholics from the South. The trip was a pilgrimage to Catholic sites in Paris, Lisbon, Lourdes, and Rome, where O'Connor met the Pope after a mass held in St. Peter's Cathedral. At the prompting of a friend, she visited the baths in Lourdes, purported to have healing powers. Upon returning home, she wrote to Hester that the baths must have worked; her hip bone was beginning to recalcify and she was no longer entirely dependent on crutches.

Despite these improvements, the condition of O'Connor's health was erratic, and she was forced to cancel a number of speaking engagements because she was too sick to travel. However, she remained hard at work on her second novel, *The Violent Bear It Away.* Soon after New Year's Day in 1959, she completed the first draft. After asking several of her close friends to read it critically—it was her usual practice to seek criticism from other writers—she made her final revisions, and the book was published in January 1960. As had been the case with *Wise Blood,* the reviews were mixed: There was a positive article in the *Atlantic Monthly,* but only a "nasty half-paragraph" in the *New Yorker.* By this point in her career, O'Connor was prepared for poor reviews and had resolved not to let them determine her worth. As she wrote to Andrew Lytle, "I expect [the novel] to get trounced but that won't make any difference if it really does work. There are not many people whose opinion on this I set store by."

Regardless of any unfavorable reviews, O'Connor's status as a writer continued to rise, both locally—in her hometown she was known as "that girl who writes"—and internationally. Her work was starting to be published in England, Germany, and France; "The Life You Save May Be Your Own" was made into a national television movie; and she was the recipient of an $8,000 Ford Foundation grant. In 1963 she was awarded an honorary degree from Smith College.

Unfortunately, around this same time, symptoms of her declining health began to appear, the worst of these being frequent fainting spells caused by anemia. Medication temporarily staved off the problem, but in February, 1964, she learned that her anemia was caused by a benign but debilitating fibroid tumor. An operation removed the tumor, but exacerbated the lupus.

Although O'Connor spoke lightly about her illness to friends, the urgency with which she worked on her writing suggests that she suspected the seriousness of her condition. Her chief concern was to finish her latest collection of stories, *Everything That Rises Must Converge*. It was during this year, the last year of her life, that three of her most critically acclaimed stories were written: "Revelation," which received first prize in the O. Henry awards, "Judgement Day," and "Parker's Back." Many of these stories she wrote longhand while lying in a hospital bed. Although she was suffering from a variety of painful ailments, O'Connor retained her unique sense of humor. In a letter written to Betty Hester months before her death, O'Connor joked that

> One of my nurses was a dead ringer for Mrs. Turpin [from "Revelation"]. Her Claud was named Otis. She told me all the time what a good nurse she was. Her favorite grammatical construction was "it were.". . . I seldom know in any given circumstances whether the Lord is giving me a reward or a punishment. She didn't know she was funny and it was agony to laugh and I reckon she increased my pain about 100%.

In July she received Extreme Unction, now called the Sacrament of the Sick, at her own request. Later that month, she was taken to Baldwin County Hospital in Milledgeville, where she died in a coma on August 3, at the age of thirty-nine. Her collection of stories, *Everything That Rises Must Converge*, was published posthumously in 1965. *The Complete Stories*, a compilation of every story she had ever written, was published in 1972 and won the National Book Award.

Upon O'Connor's death, literary magazines and Catholic periodicals received a deluge of articles written by bereaved friends and readers. Poet Elizabeth Bishop wrote that "I am sure her few books will live on and on in American literature. They are narrow, possibly, but they are hard, clear, vivid, and full of bits of description, phrases, and an odd insight that contains more real poetry than a dozen books of poems." But perhaps the most eloquent eulogy came from Catholic novelist Thomas Merton, who stated that he would not compare her with writers such as Ernest Hemingway, Katherine Ann Porter, and Jean Paul Sartre, but rather with "someone like Sophocles . . . I write her name with honor, for all the truth and all the craft with which she shows man's fall and his dishonor."

CHAPTER 1

An Introduction to Flannery O'Connor

The First Great Modern Writer from the South

Alice Walker

Alice Walker is the author of several works of fiction and poetry, including *The Color Purple*, which won an American Book Award and the Pulitzer Prize. In the subsequent article, she explains why she considers O'Connor to be "the first great modern writer from the South." Walker discusses how O'Connor's treatment of racial issues, sense of humor, and devotion to Catholicism contribute to the overall power of her work.

It was after a poetry reading I gave at a recently desegregated college in Georgia that someone mentioned that in 1952 Flannery O'Connor and I had lived within minutes of each other on the same Eatonton-to-Milledgeville road. I was eight years old in 1952 (she would have been 28) and we moved away from Milledgeville after less than a year. Still, since I have loved her work for many years, the coincidence of our having lived near each other intrigued me, and started me thinking of her again.

As a college student in the sixties I read her books endlessly, scarcely conscious of the difference between her racial and economic background and my own, but put them away in anger when I discovered that, while I was reading O'Connor—Southern, Catholic, and white—there were other women writers—some Southern, some religious, all black—I had not been allowed to know. For several years, while I searched for, found, and studied black women writers, I deliberately shut O'Connor out, feeling almost ashamed that she had reached me first. And yet, even when I no longer read her, I missed her, and realized that though the rest of America might not mind, having endured it so long, I would never be satisfied with a segregated literature. I would have to read Zora Hurston *and* Flannery O'Connor, Nella Larsen *and* Carson McCullers, Jean Toomer *and* William Faulkner, before I could begin to feel *well* read at all.

I thought it might be worthwhile, in 1974, to visit the two houses, Flannery O'Connor's and mine, to see what could be learned twenty-two years after we moved away and ten years after her death. It seemed right to go to my old house first—to set the priorities of vision, so to speak—and then to her house, to see, at the very least, whether her peacocks would still be around. To this bit of nostalgic exploration I invited my mother, who, curious about peacocks and abandoned houses, if not about literature and writers, accepted.

In her shiny new car, which at sixty-one she has learned to drive, we cruised down the wooded Georgia highway to revisit our past.

At the turnoff leading to our former house, we face a fence, a gate, a NO TRESPASSING sign. The car will not fit through the gate and beyond the gate is muddy pasture. It shocks me to remember that when we lived here we lived, literally, in a pasture. It is a memory I had repressed. Now, for a moment, it frightens me.

"Do you think we should enter?" I ask.

But my mother has already opened the gate. To her, life has no fences, except, perhaps, religious ones, and these we have decided not to discuss. We walk through pines rich with vines, fluttering birds, and an occasional wild azalea showing flashes of orange. The day is bright with spring, the sky cloudless, the road rough and clean.

"I would like to see old man Jenkins [who was our land-lord] come bothering me about some trespassing," she says, her head extremely up. "He never did pay us for the crop we made for him in fifty-two."

After five minutes of leisurely walking, we are again confronted with a fence, fastened gate, POSTED signs. Again my mother ignores all three, unfastens the gate, walks through.

"He never gave me my half of the calves I raised that year either," she says. And I chuckle at her memory and her style.

Now we are facing a large green rise. To our left calves are grazing; beyond them there are woods. To our right there is the barn we used, looking exactly as it did twenty-two years ago. It is high and weathered silver and from it comes the sweet scent of peanut hay. In front of it, a grove of pecans. Directly in front of us over the rise is what is left of the house.

"Well," says my mother, "it's still standing. And," she adds with wonder, "just look at my daffodils!"

In twenty-two years they have multiplied and are now blooming from one side of the yard to the other. It is a typical abandoned sharefarmer shack. Of the four-room house only two rooms are left; the others have rotted away. These two are filled with hay.

Considering the sad state of the house it is amazing how beautiful its setting is. There is not another house in sight. There are hills, green pastures, a ring of bright trees, and a family of rabbits hopping out of our way. My mother and I stand in the yard remembering. I remember only misery: going to a shabby segregated school that was once the state prison and that had, on the second floor, the large circular print of the electric chair that had stood there; almost stepping on a water moccasin on my way home from carrying water to my family in the fields; losing Phoebe, my cat, because we left this place hurriedly and she could not be found in time.

"Well, old house," my mother says, smiling in such a way that I almost see her rising, physically, above it, "one good thing you gave us. It was right here that I got my first washing machine!"

In fact, the only pleasant thing I recall from that year was a field we used to pass on our way into the town of Milledgeville. It was like a painting by someone who loved tranquillity. In the foreground near the road the green field was used as pasture for black-and-white cows that never seemed to move. Then, farther away, there was a steep hill partly covered with kudzu—dark and lush and creeping up to cover and change fantastically the shapes of the trees. . . . When we drive past it now, it looks the same. Even the cows could be the same cows—though now I see that they *do* move, though not very fast and never very far.

What I liked about this field as a child was that in my life of nightmares about electrocutions, lost cats, and the surprise appearances of snakes, it represented beauty and unchanging peace.

"Of course," I say to myself, as we turn off the main road two miles from my old house, "that's Flannery's field." The instructions I've been given place her house on the hill just beyond it.

There is a garish new Holiday Inn directly across Highway 441 from Flannery O'Connor's house, and, before going up to the house, my mother and I decide to have something to eat there. Twelve years ago I could not have bought lunch for us at such a place in Georgia, and I feel a weary delight as I help my mother off with her sweater and hold out a chair by the window for her. The white people eating lunch all around us—staring though trying hard not to—form a blurred backdrop against which my mother's face is especially sharp. *This* is the proper perspective, I think, biting into a corn muffin; no doubt about it.

As we sip iced tea we discuss O'Connor, integration, the inferiority of the corn muffins we are nibbling, and the care and raising of peacocks.

"Those things will sure eat up your flowers," my mother says, explaining why she never raised any.

"Yes," I say, "but they're a lot prettier than they'd be if somebody human had made them, which is why this lady

THE POWER OF O'CONNOR'S WRITING

In describing the power of Flannery O'Connor's fiction, literary critics frequently focus on her provocative subjects of damnation, prophecy, and revelation. However, Michael Kowalewski, a faculty member at Carleton College in Minnesota, asserts that O'Connor's true greatness originates from her unique—and often surreal—writing style.

It has been too frequently assumed, however, that the greatness of O'Connor's fiction resides in her subjects—sin, damnation, and prophecy—rather than in the writing which makes them take on an odd, foreboding life. An overemphasis upon the religious dimension of O'Connor's work (whether by those celebrating or dismissing it) has in many ways weakened our understanding of her fiction's capacity for making other writing seem like "roast beef." Criticism often simply seems incapable of acknowledging the full power of moments like this one, early in "The Lame Shall Enter First":

> That afternoon Norton was alone in the house, squatting on the floor of his room arranging packages of flower seeds in rows around himself. Rain slashed against the window panes and rattled in the gutters. The room had grown dark but every few minutes it was lit by silent lightning and the seed packages showed up gaily on the floor. He squatted motionless like a large pale frog in the midst of this potential garden. All at once his eyes became alert. Without warning the rain had stopped.

liked them." This idea has only just occurred to me, but having said it, I believe it is true. I sit wondering why I called Flannery O'Connor a lady. It is a word I rarely use and usually by mistake, since the whole notion of ladyhood is repugnant to me. I can imagine O'Connor at a Southern social affair, looking very polite and being very bored, making mental notes of the absurdities of the evening. Being white she would automatically have been eligible for ladyhood, but I cannot believe she would ever really have joined.

"She must have been a Christian person then," says my mother. "She believed He made everything." She pauses, looks at me with tolerance but also as if daring me to object: "And she was *right*, too."

"She was a Catholic," I say, "which must not have been comfortable in the Primitive Baptist South, and more than any other writer she believed in everything, including things she couldn't see."

> The silence was heavy as if the downpour had been hushed by violence. He remained motionless, only his eyes turning.
>
> Into the silence came the distinct click of a key turning in the front door lock . . .

Rain seldom just falls in O'Connor's fiction: it slashes or splatters or in some way comes down in a befouling, thickened state more like paint than water and less like either than, say, varnish or creosote. But the unmistakable O'Connor touch here resides not in the verbs but in the surreal reach of the similes, which transform what might otherwise be a fairly innocent scene into one of humorous grotesquerie and impending violence. We're in a world where gothic clichés (flashing lightning, hushed silence, a turning key) are simultaneously used and parodied, a world where Poe's Roderick Usher meets Emerson's transparent eyeball in the form of a "large pale frog."

The fact that we may not know exactly what a large pale frog looks like (except, perhaps, in an illustrated children's book) or that we seldom conceive of rain as being obligated to "warn" us it is preparing to stop, seems to have little to do with the evocative power of this kind of writing. Or rather, such odd conceits don't depend for their power upon our knowing or even pretending to know what in the world they might "mean."

Michael Kowalewski, "On Flannery O'Connor," *Raritan*, Winter 1991.

"Is that why you like her?" she asks.

"I like her because she could *write*," I say.

"'Flannery' sounds like something to eat," someone said to me once. The word always reminds me of flannel, the material used to make nightgowns and winter shirts. It is very Irish, as were her ancestors. Her first name was Mary, but she seems never to have used it. Certainly "Mary O'Connor" is short on mystery. She was an Aries, born March 25, 1925. When she was sixteen, her father died of lupus, the disease that, years later, caused her own death. After her father died, O'Connor and her mother, Regina O'Connor, moved from Savannah, Georgia, to Milledgeville, where they lived in a townhouse built for Flannery O'Connor's grandfather, Peter Cline. This house, called "the Cline house," was built by slaves who made the bricks by hand. O'Connor's biographers are always impressed by this fact, as if it adds the blessed sign of aristocracy, but whenever I read it I think that those slaves were some of my own relatives, toiling in the stifling middle-Georgia heat, to erect her grandfather's house, sweating and suffering the swarming mosquitoes as the house rose slowly, brick by brick.

Whenever I visit antebellum homes in the South, with their spacious rooms, their grand staircases, their shaded back windows that, without the thickly planted trees, would look out onto the now vanished slave quarters in the back, this is invariably my thought. I stand in the backyard gazing up at the windows, then stand at the windows inside looking down into the backyard, and between the me that is on the ground and the me that is at the windows, History is caught.

O'Connor attended local Catholic schools and then Georgia Women's College. In 1945 she received a fellowship to the Writer's Workshop at the University of Iowa. She received her M.A. in 1947. While still a student she wrote stories that caused her to be recognized as a writer of formidable talent and integrity of craft. After a stay at Yaddo, the artists' colony in upstate New York, she moved to a furnished room in New York City. Later she lived and wrote over a garage at the Connecticut home of Sally and Robert Fitzgerald, who became, after her death, her literary executors.

Although, as Robert Fitzgerald states in the preface to O'Connor's *Everything That Rises Must Converge*, "Flannery was out to be a writer on her own and had no plans to go back to live in Georgia," staying out of Georgia for good was not possible. In December of 1950 she experienced a peculiar heaviness in her "typing arms." On the train home for the Christmas holidays she became so ill she was hospitalized immediately. It was disseminated lupus. In the fall of 1951, after nine wretched months in the hospital, she returned to Milledgeville. Because she could not climb the stairs at the Cline house her mother brought her to their country house, Andalusia, about five miles from town. Flannery O'Connor lived there with her mother for the next thirteen years. The rest of her life.

The word *lupus* is Latin for "wolf," and is described as "that which eats into the substance." It is a painful, wasting disease, and O'Connor suffered not only from the disease— which caused her muscles to weaken and her body to swell, among other things—but from the medicine she was given to fight the disease, which caused her hair to fall out and her hipbones to melt. Still, she managed—with the aid of crutches from 1955 on—to get about and to write, and left behind more than three dozen superb short stories, most of them prizewinners, two novels, and a dozen or so brilliant essays and speeches. Her book of essays, *Mystery and Manners*, which is primarily concerned with the moral imperatives of the serious writer of fiction, is the best of its kind I have ever read.

"When you make these trips back south," says my mother, as I give the smiling waitress my credit card, "just what is it exactly that you're looking for?"

"A wholeness," I reply.

"You look whole enough to me," she says.

"No," I answer, "because everything around me is split up, deliberately split up. History split up, literature split up, and people are split up too. It makes people do ignorant things. For example, one day I was invited to speak at a gathering of Mississippi librarians and before I could get started, one of the authorities on Mississippi history and literature got up and said she really *did* think Southerners wrote so well because 'we' lost the war. She was white, of course, but half the librarians in the room were black."

"I bet she was real old," says my mother. "They're the only ones still worrying over that war."

"So I got up and said no, 'we' didn't lose the war. '*You* all' lost the war. And you all's loss was our gain."

"Those old ones will just have to die out," says my mother.

"Well," I say, "I believe that the truth about any subject only comes when all the sides of the story are put together, and all their different meanings make one new one. Each writer writes the missing parts to the other writer's story. And the whole story is what I'm after."

"Well, I doubt if you can ever get the *true* missing parts of anything away from the white folks," my mother says softly, so as not to offend the waitress who is mopping up a nearby table; "they've sat on the truth so long by now they've mashed the life out of it."

"O'Connor wrote a story once called 'Everything That Rises Must Converge.'"

"What?"

"Everything that goes up comes together, meets, becomes one thing. Briefly, the story is this: an old white woman in her fifties—"

"That's not old! I'm older than that, and I'm not old!"

"Sorry. This middle-aged woman gets on a bus with her son, who likes to think he is a Southern liberal . . . he looks for a black person to sit next to. This horrifies his mother, who, though not old, has old ways. She is wearing a very hideous, very expensive hat, which is purple and green."

"Purple and *green*?"

"Very expensive. *Smart*. Bought at the best store in town. She says, 'With a hat like this, I won't meet myself coming and going.' But in fact, soon a large black woman whom O'Connor describes as looking something like a gorilla, gets on the bus with a little boy, and she is wearing this same green-and-purple hat. Well, our not-so-young white lady is horrified, out*done*."

"I *bet* she was. Black folks have money to buy foolish things with too, now."

"O'Connor's point exactly! Everything that rises, must converge."

"Well, the green-and-purple-hats people will have to converge without me."

"O'Connor thought that the South, as it became more 'progressive,' would become just like the North. Culturally bland, physically ravished, and, where the people are concerned, well, you wouldn't be able to tell one racial group from another. Everybody would want the same things, like the same things, and everybody would be reduced to wearing, symbolically, the same green-and-purple hats."

"And do you think this is happening?"

"I do. But that is not the whole point of the story. The white woman, in an attempt to save her pride, chooses to treat the incident of the identical hats as a case of monkey-see, monkey-do. She assumes she is not the monkey, of course. She ignores the idiotic-looking black woman and begins instead to flirt with the woman's son, who is small and black and *cute*. She fails to notice that the black woman is glowering at her. When they all get off the bus she offers the little boy a 'bright new penny.' And the child's mother knocks the hell out of her with her pocketbook."

"I bet she carried a large one."

"Large, and full of hard objects."

"Then what happened? Didn't you say the white woman's son was with her?"

"He had tried to warn his mother. 'These new Negroes are not like the old,' he told her. But she never listened. He thought he hated his mother until he saw her on the ground, then he felt sorry for her. But when he tried to help her, she didn't know him. She'd retreated in her mind to a historical time more congenial to her desires. 'Tell Grandpapa to come get me,' she says. Then she totters off, alone, into the night."

"Poor *thing*," my mother says sympathetically of this horrid woman, in a total identification that is so Southern and so black.

"That's what her son felt, too, and *that* is how you know it is a Flannery O'Connor story. The son has been changed by his mother's experience. He understands that, though she is a silly woman who has tried to live in the past, she is also a pathetic creature and so is he. But it is too late to tell her about this because she is stone crazy."

"What did the black woman do after she knocked the white woman down and walked away?"

"O'Connor chose not to say, and that is why, although this is a good story, it is, to me, only half a story. *You* might know the other half. . . ."

"Well, I'm not a writer, but there *was* an old white woman I once wanted to strike . . ." she begins.

"Exactly," I say.

I discovered O'Connor when I was in college in the North and took a course in Southern writers and the South. The perfection of her writing was so dazzling I never noticed that no black Southern writers were taught. The other writers we studied—Faulkner, McCullers, Welty—seemed obsessed with a racial past that would not let them go. They seemed to beg the question of their characters' humanity on every page. O'Connor's characters—whose humanity if not their sanity is taken for granted, and who are miserable, ugly, narrow-minded, atheistic, and of intense racial smugness and arrogance, with not a graceful, pretty one anywhere who is not, at the same time, a joke—shocked and delighted me.

It was for her description of Southern white women that I appreciated her work at first, because when she set her pen to them not a whiff of magnolia hovered in the air (and the tree itself might never have been planted), and yes, I could say, yes, these white folks without the magnolia (who are indifferent to the tree's existence), and these black folks without melons and superior racial patience, these are like Southerners that I know.

THE FIRST GREAT MODERN WRITER FROM THE SOUTH

She was for me the first great modern writer from the South, and was, in any case, the only one I had read who wrote such sly, demythifying sentences about white women as: "The woman would be more or less pretty—yellow hair, fat ankles, muddy-colored eyes."

Her white male characters do not fare any better—all of them misfits, thieves, deformed madmen, idiot children, illiterates, and murderers, and her black characters, male and female, appear equally shallow, demented, and absurd. That she retained a certain distance (only, however, in her later, mature work) from the inner workings of her black characters seems to me all to her credit, since, by deliberately limiting her treatment of them to cover their observable demeanor and actions, she leaves them free, in the reader's imagination, to inhabit another landscape, another life, than the one she creates for them. This is a kind of grace many writers do not have when dealing with representatives of an oppressed people within a story, and their insistence on knowing everything, on being God, in fact, has burdened us with more stereotypes than we can ever hope to shed.

In her life, O'Connor was more casual. In a letter to her friend Robert Fitzgerald in the mid-fifties she wrote, "as the niggers say, I have the misery." He found nothing offensive, apparently, in including this unflattering (to O'Connor) statement in his Introduction to one of her books. O'Connor was then certain she was dying, and was in pain; one assumes she made this comment in an attempt at levity. Even so, I do not find it funny. In another letter she wrote shortly before she died she said: "Justice is justice and should not be appealed to along racial lines. The problem is not abstract for the Southerner, it's concrete: he sees it in terms of persons, not races—which way of seeing does away with easy answers." Of course this observation, though grand, does not apply to the racist treatment of blacks by whites in the South, and O'Connor should have added that she spoke only for herself.

But *essential* O'Connor is not about race at all, which is why it is so refreshing, coming, as it does, out of such a *racial* culture. If it can be said to be "about" anything, then it is "about" prophets and prophecy, "about" revelation, and "about" the impact of supernatural grace on human beings who don't have a chance of spiritual growth without it.

An indication that *she* believed in justice for the individual (if only in the corrected portrayal of a character she invented) is shown by her endless reworking of "The Geranium," the first story she published (in 1946), when she was twenty-one. She revised the story several times, renamed it at least twice, until, nearly twenty years after she'd originally published it (and significantly, I think, after the beginning of the Civil Rights Movement), it became a different tale. Her two main black characters, a man and a woman, underwent complete metamorphosis.

In the original story, Old Dudley, a senile racist from the South, lives with his daughter in a New York City building that has "niggers" living in it too. The black characters are described as being passive, self-effacing people. The black woman sits quietly, hands folded, in her apartment; the man, her husband, helps Old Dudley up the stairs when the old man is out of breath, and chats with him kindly, if condescendingly, about guns and hunting. But in the final version of the story, the woman walks around Old Dudley (now called Tanner) as if he's an open bag of garbage, scowls whenever she sees him, and "didn't look like any kind of woman, black or white, he had ever seen." Her husband, whom Old Dudley persists in calling "Preacher" (under the misguided assumption that to all black men it is a courtesy title), twice knocks the old man down. At the end of the story he stuffs Old Dudley's head, arms, and legs through the banisters of the stairway "as if in a stockade," and leaves him to die. The story's final title is "Judgment Day."

The quality added is rage, and, in this instance, O'Connor waited until she saw it *exhibited* by black people before she recorded it.

O'CONNOR'S HUMOR

She was an artist who thought she might die young, and who then knew for certain she would. Her view of her characters pierces right through to the skull. Whatever her characters' color or social position she saw them as she saw herself, in the light of imminent mortality. Some of her stories, "The Enduring Chill" and "The Comforts of Home" especially, seem to be written out of the despair that must, on occasion, have come from this bleak vision, but it is for her humor that she is most enjoyed and remembered. My favorites are these:

> Everywhere I go I'm asked if I think the universities stifle writers. My opinion is that they don't stifle enough of them. There's many a best-seller that could have been prevented by a good teacher.
>
> —MYSTERY AND MANNERS

> "She would of been a good woman, if it had been somebody there to shoot her every minute of her life."
>
> —"The Misfit,"
>   A GOOD MAN IS HARD TO FIND

> There are certain cases in which, if you can only learn to write poorly enough, you can make a great deal of money.
>
> —MYSTERY AND MANNERS

> It is the business of fiction to embody mystery through manners, and mystery is a great embarrassment to the modern mind.
>
> —MYSTERY AND MANNERS

It mattered to her that she was a Catholic. This comes as a surprise to those who first read her work as that of an atheist. She believed in all the mysteries of her faith. And yet, she was incapable of writing dogmatic or formulaic stories. No religious tracts, nothing haloed softly in celestial light, not even any happy endings. It has puzzled some of her readers and annoyed the Catholic church that in her stories not only does good not triumph, it is not usually present. Seldom are there choices, and God never intervenes to help anyone win. To O'Connor, in fact, Jesus was God, and he won only by losing. She perceived that not much has been learned by his death by crucifixion, and that it is only by his continual, repeated dying—touching one's own life in a direct, searing way—that the meaning of that original loss is pressed into the heart of the individual.

In "The Displaced Person," a story published in 1954, a refugee from Poland is hired to work on a woman's dairy farm. Although he speaks in apparent gibberish, he is a perfect worker. He works so assiduously the woman begins to prosper beyond her greatest hopes. Still, because his ways are not her own (the Displaced Person attempts to get one of the black dairy workers to marry his niece by "buying" her out of a Polish concentration camp), the woman allows a runaway tractor to roll over and kill him.

As far as I'm concerned," she tells the priest, "Christ was just another D.P." He just didn't fit in. After the death of the Polish refugee, however, she understands her complicity in a modern crucifixion, and recognizes the enormity of her responsibility for other human beings. The impact of this new awareness debilitates her; she loses her health, her farm, even her ability to speak.

This moment of revelation, when the individual comes face to face with her own limitations and comprehends "the true frontiers of her own inner country," is classic O'Connor, and always arrives in times of extreme crisis and loss.

RESISTANCE TO READING O'CONNOR

There is a resistance by some to read O'Connor because she is "too difficult," or because they do not share her religious "persuasion." A young man who studied O'Connor under the direction of Eudora Welty some years ago amused me with the following story, which may or may not be true:

"I don't think Welty and O'Connor understood each *other*," he said, when I asked if he thought O'Connor would have liked or understood Welty's more conventional art. "For Welty's part, wherever we reached a particularly dense and symbolic section of one of O'Connor's stories she would sigh and ask, 'Is there a Catholic in the class?'"

Whether one "understands" her stories or not, one knows her characters are new and wondrous creations in the world and that not one of her stories—not even the earliest ones in which her consciousness of racial matters had not evolved sufficiently to be interesting or to differ much from the insulting and ignorant racial stereotyping that preceded it—could have been written by anyone else. As one can tell a Bearden from a Keene or a Picasso from a Hallmark card, one can tell an O'Connor story from any story laid next to it. Her Catholicism did not in any way limit (by defining it) her art. After her great stories of sin, damnation, prophecy, and revelation, the stories one reads casually in the average magazine seem to be about love and roast beef.

Andalusia is a large white house at the top of a hill with a view of a lake from its screened-in front porch. It is neatly kept, and there are, indeed, peacocks strutting about in the sun. Behind it there is an unpainted house where black people must have lived. It was, then, the typical middle-to-upper-class arrangement: white folks up front, the "help," in a far shabbier house, within calling distance from the back door. Although an acquaintance of O'Connor's has told me no one lives there now—but that a caretaker looks after things—I go up to the porch and knock. It is not an entirely empty or symbolic gesture: I have come to this vacant house to learn something about myself in relation to Flannery O'Connor, and will learn it whether anyone is home or not.

What I feel at the moment of knocking is fury that someone is paid to take care of her house, though no one lives in it, and that her house still, in fact, stands, while mine—which of course we never owned anyway—is slowly rotting into dust. Her house becomes—in an instant—the symbol of my own disinheritance, and for that instant I hate her guts. All that she has meant to me is diminished, though her diminishment within me is against my will.

In Faulkner's backyard there is also an unpainted shack and a black caretaker still lives there, a quiet, somber man who, when asked about Faulkner's legendary "sense of humor" replied that as far as he knew, "Mr. Bill never joked." For years, while reading Faulkner, this image of the quiet man in the backyard shack stretched itself across the page.

Standing there knocking on Flannery O'Connor's door, I do not think of her illness, her magnificent work in spite of it; I think: it all comes back to houses. To how people live. There are rich people who own houses to live in and poor people who do not. And this is wrong. Literary separatism, fashionable now among blacks as it has always been among whites, is easier to practice than to change a fact like this. I think: I would level this country with the sweep of my hand, if I could.

"Nobody can change the past," says my mother.

"Which is why revolutions exist," I reply.

My bitterness comes from a deeper source than my knowledge of the difference, historically, race has made in the lives of white and black artists. The fact that in Mississippi no one even remembers where Richard Wright lived, while Faulkner's house is maintained by a black caretaker is painful, but not unbearable. What comes close to being unbearable is that I know how damaging to my own psyche such injustice is. In an unjust society the soul of the sensitive person is in danger of deformity from just such weights as this. For a long time I will feel Faulkner's house, O'Connor's house, crushing me. To fight back will require a certain amount of energy, energy better used doing something else.

My mother has been busy reasoning that, since Flannery O'Connor died young of a lingering and painful illness, the hand of God has shown itself. Then she sighs. "Well, you know," she says, "it is true, as they say, that the grass is always greener on the other side. That is, until you find yourself over there."

In a just society, of course, clichés like this could not survive.

"But grass *can* be greener on the other side and not be just an illusion," I say. "Grass on the other side of the fence might have good fertilizer, while grass on your side might have to grow, if it grows at all, in sand."

We walk about quietly, listening to the soft sweep of the peacocks' tails as they move across the yard. I notice how completely O'Connor, in her fiction, has described just this view of the rounded hills, the tree line, black against the sky, the dirt road that runs from the front yard down to the highway. I remind myself of her courage and of how much—in her art—she has helped me to see. She destroyed the last vestiges of sentimentality in white Southern writing; she caused white women to look ridiculous on pedestals, and she approached her black characters—as a mature artist—with unusual humility and restraint. She also cast spells and worked magic with the written word. The magic, the wit, and the mystery of Flannery O'Connor I know I will always love, I also know the meaning of the expression "Take what you can use and let the rest rot." If ever there was an expression designed to protect the health of the spirit, this is it.

As we leave O'Connor's yard the peacocks—who she said would have the last word—lift their splendid tails for our edification. One peacock is so involved in the presentation of his masterpiece he does not allow us to move the car until he finishes with his show.

"Peacocks are inspiring," I say to my mother, who does not seem at all in awe of them and actually frowns when she sees them strut, "but they sure don't stop to consider they might be standing in your way."

And she says, "Yes, and they'll eat up every bloom you have, if you don't watch out."

O'Connor's Challenge to Her Readers

Marilyn Chandler McEntyre

In most of O'Connor's stories, a violent incident causes her characters to experience a moment of epiphany. Marilyn Chandler McEntyre argues in the following selection that O'Connor's objective is to provoke her readers to recognize the evil in the world and their own need for redemption. McEntyre, associate professor of English at Westmont College in Santa Barbara, is the author of *Dwelling in the Text: Houses in American Fiction* and *A Healing Art: Regeneration Through Autobiography.*

In one of Flannery O'Connor's best-known stories, a surly adolescent sets fire to his great uncle's farm and abandons the corpse of the uncle he promised to bury. In the same story, he drowns a young child in the act of baptizing him. Thereafter, he himself is a victim of homosexual rape. In another of her stories, a grandfather smashes his favorite grandchild's head on a rock in a struggle that has taken both beyond all inhibition. In another, a grandmother, her son, his wife, and three grandchildren are shot point-blank in a ditch by the side of the road. In another, an old man is stuffed between the bannister rails of his apartment building and left to die. In another, a widow is gored by a bull. The inventory could go on to include most of O'Connor's thirty short stories and novellas. In almost every tale, an implied epiphany is preceded or accompanied by an act of violence.

The fact of violence in fiction is certainly nothing new to readers raised in a media culture in which violence has become a cliché. What is surprising in O'Connor's stories is how she upends and indicts the clichés, the trivialization of violence, and the sentimentalities that soften our vision and confuse our judgment of it. Her objective, and her success, is

Excerpted from "Mercy That Burns: Violence and Revelation in Flannery O'Connor's Fiction," by Marilyn Chandler McEntyre, *Theology Today*, October 1996.

to restore to a largely jaded audience the capacity for shock and with that, the possibility of recognizing evil, our involvement in it, and our need for redemption. She does this not by racheting up sensationalistic effects but by taking an insistently theological view of human action and motive that refuses to make sin a function simply of improper social conditioning, or evil a romantic idea. Her protagonists commit crimes, hate their neighbors, and wallow in bigotry, but they are not the antiheroes of other contemporary fiction. Nor are the objects of their hostilities sympathetic victims. Perhaps one of the truest general observations about O'Connor's characters is that none of them is likeable. Though some of them evoke laughter, there are none with whom any respectable reader would readily and wholeheartedly identify. One of the several biblical truths her stories serve to illuminate is that all have sinned, that there is none righteous, no not one.

O'CONNOR'S CAST OF CHARACTERS

Let us pause for a moment to survey her cast of characters. There are the "good country people"—insouciant rednecks whose prejudices organize the world for them. There are self-styled prophets and backwoods preachers whose energies are devoted either to vitriolically brandishing the Word of God in the face of their fellows or, Jonah-like, attempting to escape what they believe to be the call of God by railing against God. There are sullen adolescents (sometimes upwards of thirty years old) whose unrighteous judgment of their unenlightened elders simply substitutes one form of moral hubris for another. There are "duty-proud" women who preen themselves on their conspicuous and unrelenting forms of maternal or filial self-sacrifice. There are the deformed, the disfigured, the demented, and the maimed—afflicted and poor, but without socially redeeming sentimental appeal. There are the fixtures of Southern fiction: "white trash" and "niggers"—so called by the many characters who expend considerable energy avoiding any kind of contact with those two classes that might disorganize their fixed ideas about them. There are city dwellers reminiscent of [writer T.S.] Eliot's "hollow men"—social scientists, social workers, self-assured secular-scientific do-gooders who leave the reader ready to run for refreshment back to the ranting prophets in the woods. There are "sluts" and thieves and murderers. And there are, occasionally, Catholics, who show up against the double backdrop of revivalist Bible Christians and sneering atheists as anomalous in their own right.

All of these people are odd or repellent. But we discover, perhaps to our chagrin, that we can't condemn any of them outright without finding ourselves in the camp of some of their equally objectionable compatriots. O'Connor's genius is that despite our natural repugnance, we do identify with them. And the moment we allow ourselves to grasp them from the inside is a salutary moment of acknowledgement that brings us to renewed recognition of our own flawed characters and sinfulness.

This is hardly a comfortable state in which to find ourselves. If the function of good fiction may be defined in the way Robert McAfee Brown once defined the function of good teaching—to comfort the afflicted and afflict the comfortable—O'Connor puts by far the heavier stress on the latter half of that equation. But the discomfort and horror with which she afflicts us are not gratuitous, certainly not an indulgence in the perverse for its sensationalistic effects. She acknowledges that first of all what readers need and want is "to be lifted up." "There is something in us . . . ," she continues, "that demands the redemptive act, that demands that what falls at least be offered the chance to be restored. The reader of today looks for this motion, and rightly so, but what he has forgotten is the cost of it. His sense of evil is diluted or lacking altogether, and so he has forgotten the price of restoration."

In literature courses, I frequently open discussion of a work of fiction by asking the students to consider what the writer is asking of them. O'Connor asks a great deal. She challenges her readers to take on some of the most intellectually baffling and emotionally disturbing aspects of Christian faith. "I see from the standpoint of Christian orthodoxy," she writes. "This means that for me the meaning of life is centered in our Redemption by Christ and what I see in the world I see in its relation to that. I don't think that this is a position that can be taken halfway or one that is particularly easy in these times to make transparent in fiction." O'Connor sees "these times" primarily in terms of atrophied faith and dulled sensibilities. We have become a people, she implies, dwelling in a gray haze of mass culture where the glitter of the manufactured blinds us to the beauty of the natural and where sentimentality and obscenity (which she takes to be flip sides of the same thing) are the currency of public discourse. In her stories, the city is a scene of corruption. But the country is not correspondingly a place of purification. Nature is not redemptive in itself; the sentimentalization of nature is one of many romantic fallacies for which she has no respect. . . .

THE "HARD SAYINGS" OF SCRIPTURE

The truth O'Connor's stories tell is grounded most conspicuously in the "hard sayings" of Scripture. Far from attempting to make Christianity accessible, comprehensible, or palatable to a contemporary audience, she goes to the most baffling and troubling of its claims and challenges us to begin our reflection there. Think, for instance, of the harsh admonishment, "all our righteousnesses are as filthy rags" (Isa. 64:6b). To accept that as a truth requires a radical reordering of our understanding of human values and notions of the virtuous life. This verse might well serve as an epigraph to three stories in particular, . . . in which nice, decent ladies, conscious of their faithful performance of Christian duty toward those lower than they, embody the particular brand of pharisaism O'Connor confronted at intimate distance among her mother's peers.

Mrs. Turpin, for instance, in "Revelation" silently sizes up each fellow occupant of a doctor's waiting room in order to reaffirm, with gratitude to Jesus, with whom she is in frequent conversation, her own general superiority. She compares herself to those around her to reassure herself of the many ways she's been particularly blessed, especially in being such a good person. "To help anybody out that needed it was her philosophy of life. She never spared herself when she found somebody in need, whether they were white or black, trash or decent. And of all that she had to be thankful for, she was most thankful that this was so." She may be fat, she reasons, but she has better skin than the scowling girl whose face, bent balefully over a book called *Human Development*, is "blue with acne." And she knows more about raising children than the "white-trash" lady who has come into public in bedroom slippers and doesn't bother to tell her lethargic child to give his seat to the lady. And of course, she knows better than her docile husband, Claud, what's good for him. Mrs. Turpin's moral reasoning consists of imagined conversations with Jesus in which he confronts her with a choice. She considers, for instance:

> If Jesus had said to her before he made her, "There's only two places available for you. You can either be a nigger or white-trash," what would she have said? "Please, Jesus, please," she would have said, "just let me wait until there's another place available," and he would have said, "No, you have to go right now and I have only those two places so make up your mind." She would have wiggled and squirmed and begged and pleaded but it would have been no use and finally she would have said, "All right, make me a nigger then—but that don't mean a trashy one." And he would have made her a neat clean respectable Negro woman, herself but black.

"THE TIRED READER"

Flannery O'Connor was frustrated by letters she received from readers who sought to be uplifted by fiction and complained that her stories were too disturbing. In the following excerpt from one of her lectures, O'Connor explains the difficulty of writing for "the tired reader."

You may say that the serious writer doesn't have to bother about the tired reader, but he does, because they are all tired. One old lady who wants her heart lifted up wouldn't be so bad, but you multiply her two hundred and fifty thousand times and what you get is a book club. I used to think it should be possible to write for some supposed elite, for the people who attend universities and sometimes know how to read, but I have since found that though you may publish your stories in *Botteghe Oscure*, if they are any good at all, you are eventually going to get a letter from some old lady in California, or some inmate of the Federal Penitentiary or the state insane asylum or the local poorhouse, telling you where you have failed to meet his needs.

And his need, of course, is to be lifted up. There is something in us, as storytellers and listeners to stories, that demands the redemptive act, that demands that what falls at least be offered the chance to be restored. The reader of today looks for this motion, and rightly so, but what he has forgotten is the cost of it. His sense of evil is diluted or lacking altogether, and so he has forgotten the price of restoration. When he reads a novel, he wants either his senses tormented or his spirits raised. He wants to be transported, instantly, either to mock damnation or a mock innocence.

Flannery O'Connor, *Mystery and Manners*. New York: Farrar, Straus & Giroux, 1969.

Mrs. Turpin sees the world through a fixed grid of social categories, and her inner life consists of an endless catalogue of judgments that reaffirm those categories, her place in this world and the next, and thus her psychological security. She is not the only character who makes such fixed judgments. The "stylish lady" she targets as the only fit partner for conversation firmly pronounces on the primary importance of a "good disposition." "You just can't beat a good disposition," she observes, and she goes on to comment with the same certainty on the good weather, the punctuality of the clock, and the utility of cotton-picking machines that spare one the awkward problem of "niggers" that won't pick cotton any more because, as Mrs. Turpin points out, "they got to be right up there with the white folks." Eventually, even the "white-trash woman" enters the conversation to make her own judgment on the "pig parlor" where Mrs. Turpin keeps hogs that are "cleaner than some children I've seen." "One thang I know," she declares from her own place of superiority, "Two thangs I ain't going to do: love no niggers or scoot down no hog with no hose."

Mary Grace, the seething adolescent whose incongruous name underscores her surprising function as an instrument of grace, finally fed up with Mrs. Turpin's self-satisfied prattle, throws her book across the room, hits Mrs. Turpin over her left eye, and attacks her in a howling fit of fury. Much might be said about the symbolic significance of "throwing the book at her," but let us consider here simply the literal violence of the act. Suddenly we find our own judgment of Mrs. Turpin's annoying self-congratulation acted out with a fury that shocks us into wondering whether in fact she really deserves such excessive punishment. Isn't there, after all, a certain forgivable innocence in her complacency? Haven't we ourselves been enjoying feeling a little superior to this parochial, simplistic farm woman and her foibles, and laughing at them? Still, Mary Grace's rage must give us pause. (So might her name!) Because there is something about the Mrs. Turpins of the world that incites—and deserves—indignation. Her very virtues are imbedded in a framework of self-righteousness of the kind Jesus most severely condemned. Yet, we hardly wish to align ourselves with the ugly, mean-spirited, out-of-control adolescent who, even as we continue reading, is carted off to a psychiatric ward. If she represents the truth-sayer, do we want to acknowledge the truth she represents? You see the dilemma. We are left in the waiting room wondering with whom we ourselves might be willing to associate. Our own strategies of self-protection and devices of self-deception are mirrored back to us in "large and startling figures."

MRS. TURPIN'S REVELATION

Finally, it is Mrs. Turpin who has the "revelation" in question. In an act we are bound to recognize as both courageous and humble, She leans, looks directly into her assailant's eyes, and asks, " 'What you got to say to me?' . . . waiting, as for a revelation." The girl's reply upends everything she has believed about herself and her place in the order of things. " 'Go back to hell where you came from, you old wart hog,' " the girl hisses before they carry her out. Mrs. Turpin, whose endless gratitude that she is made just the way she is and not like other, less balanced and gracious folk, not only takes the girl's snarling epithet seriously enough to wonder what it is she saw but goes a step further. Retreating to her conversation with Jesus, she asks in anguish, " 'What do you send me a message like that for? . . . How am I a hog and me both? How am I saved and from hell too?' " Mrs. Turpin's willingness to receive this hurtful attack as a message from Jesus opens her to the action of grace. Grace comes dramatically later that day in a moment of meditation by the hog pen as the sun goes down. She sees in a vision

> a vast horde of souls . . . rumbling toward heaven. There were whole companies of white-trash, clean for the first time in their lives, and bands of black niggers in white robes and battalions of freaks and lunatics shouting and clapping and leaping like frogs. And bringing up the end of the procession was a tribe of people whom she recognized at once as those who, like herself and Claud, had always had a little of everything and the God-given wit to use it right.

These last, among whom she numbers herself, sing on key, march in good order, and comport themselves with wonted common sense and respectable behavior, yet "she could see by their shocked and altered faces that even their virtues were being burned away."

Any reader disposed to keep a comforting mental record of good works is jolted in that one phrase back to the unsettling truth that salvation comes by faith alone. Our reckonings of our own goodness are specious, misplaced, and dangerous. As Luther's profound conviction of his own sin opened the door to a joyful life of faith, so here Mrs. Turpin seems to absorb some "abysmal life-giving knowledge," painful and disorienting in the measure required to restore the plumb line of truth. We don't see her reform. We are left to speculate, but there is no question about the nature of the hope that has been offered.

The story challenges us to recognize that sin comes in many shapes, some of which seem reasonable facsimiles of Christian charity. It asks us to recognize the ugliness of sin, to identify ourselves among the sinners, and in doing so, to arrive at the possibility of loving the unloveable. It asks us to reckon with what T.S. Eliot called "things ill done or done to others' harm which once we took for exercise of virtue."

We are also compelled to laugh—first at others' folly and then, less comfortably, at our own. Because for this writer, as for Dante whom she revered, the larger frame of human action is the "divine comedy." Behind the most horrific moments of violence, pain, and defeat in her stories is the good news of mercy and grace. But it makes very few dramatic appearances like Mrs. Turpin's vision. More frequently, O'Connor's stories recall the strange, elliptical, abrupt character of the Gospel of Mark, where the good news is delivered in hints and guesses, and those who hear it are admonished to secrecy. The endings of the stories work in much the same way as the much-discussed original ending of Mark. As most scholars now acknowledge, before the last ten verses were added, the story ended on a note of amazement, fear, secrecy, and inconclusiveness (Mark 16:8). We are left with the bafflement of the original witnesses and with a narrative that, though it forcibly proclaims its own truth, seems at every turn also to take its readers by surprise and leave them mystified. . . .

THE CHALLENGE OF O'CONNOR'S FICTION

O'Connor's fiction again and again presses us on the issue of what we are willing to allow into both our minds and our hearts. How willing, or capable, are we of suspending either disbelief or judgment? Certainly, O'Connor's stories invite us to rub elbows with publicans, sinners, crazies, and outcasts with an intimacy we might just as soon avoid. They compel us to reckon with the inadequacy of our own instinctive moral judgments. They prevent us from resting comfortably with the social categories to which we are accustomed. They leave us with unsolved theological conundrums, ranging from the most elemental questions about creation and destiny to Protestant-Catholic debates about the importance of the sacraments, the uses of Scripture, and principles of interpretation. She is not a theologian, though she writes from a thoroughly theological perspective. She raises questions she doesn't attempt to solve in a systematic way, though she does very much intend them to be wrestled with. Where her stories venture into explicit theological statement, it is of a rather simple character, like the catechizing of Father Finn, disappointing in its lack of intellectual complexity to Asbury, the embittered, dying artist in "An Enduring Chill": "Do you say your morning and night prayers? . . . Well, you will never learn to be good unless you pray regularly. You cannot love Jesus unless you speak to Him." Or again, through the eyes of another simple priest, she offers us a moment of epiphany and praise. The priest's eye happens to fall on a peacock spreading its glorious tail-feathers:

> The cock stopped suddenly and curving his neck backwards, he raised his tail and spread it with a shimmering timbrous noise. Tiers of small pregnant suns floated in a green-gold haze over his head. The priest stood transfixed, his jaw slack. Mrs. McIntyre wondered where she had ever seen such an idiotic old man. "Christ will come like that!" he said in a loud gay voice and wiped his hand over his mouth and stood there, gaping.

It is easy enough to sentimentalize the idea of Christ's "little ones" or to soften and sanitize the familiar categories of the blessed: the poor, those who mourn, those who hunger and thirst, the afflicted. But to look poverty, affliction, anguish, loneliness, or even simplicity directly in the face and to realize that God really chooses the unlikeliest of instruments to work the divine will is an experience of radical discomfort. O'Connor acknowledged once to an audience that perhaps all a Christian writer could hope effectively to reflect to a modern audience, largely unbelievers, was not "the image at the heart of things" but "the face of the devil we are possessed by." This, she mused, might be "a modest achievement, but perhaps a necessary one."

O'Connor's fiction challenges us not to avert our eyes but to stand agape like the priest before the peacock or Mr. Greenleaf before the charging bull, cognizant of the limitations of all our ways of making the world explicable and safe. "I think that if there is any value in hearing writers talk," O'Connor observed at one public appearance, "it will be in hearing what they can witness to and not what they can theorize about." She leaves us with no theories, arguments, or theological position statements, but driven to reconsider our own certainties and the terms in which we know and believe. Her own approach to the mysteries of life comes very close to the one Augustine expressed when he asserted, "I believe in order to understand." Perhaps, also, in order to have the last laugh—for her fiction is full of laughter of a kind not easy to square with the horrors it purveys yet, by her reasoning, entirely in keeping with a Christian view of even a degenerate and dissolute world. "Either one is serious about salvation or one is not," she reasons. "And it is well to realize that the maximum amount of seriousness admits the maximum amount of comedy. Only if we are secure in our beliefs can we see the comical side of the universe." The laughter she invites us to in these darkly comic tales is a laughter that mocks the devil, affirms the burning mercy of God, and perhaps also reminds us of another of Augustine's claims: that the end of all things is delight.

Emblematic Moments in O'Connor's Fiction

Jill Pelaez Baumgaertner

Jill Pelaez Baumgaertner is a professor of English at Wheaton College, the poetry editor of the *Christian Century*, and the author of *Flannery O'Connor: A Proper Scaring*, from which the following article is excerpted. In this article, she states that O'Connor's stories center around "emblematic moments." At the height of a story's climax, she contends, O'Connor captures a strange picture. Baumgaertner likens these pictures to seventeenth-century emblems— visual representations of a scriptural truth.

First responses to O'Connor are invariably extreme. Forgetting about the stoning of St. Stephen or Herod's slaughter of the innocents or even the cross itself, many first-time readers of O'Connor, knowing only that she is a Christian writer, are puzzled by her grotesqueries and the violence of her vision. The problem is, of course, that most readers possess flimsy ideas about what is "Christian" literature and what is not. In a review written in 1956 O'Connor claimed that "virtue can believably triumph only in completely drawn characters and against a background whose roots are recognized to be in original sin." The characters in O'Connor's stories find grace, but between their flight from the City of Destruction and their arrival at the gates of the Heavenly City, they must encounter the trauma of the cross.

No matter how you read it, the gospel contains birth in a cold, dirty stable and violent death on Golgotha. The Incarnation finds its actual fulfillment in the Resurrection, but resurrection requires death. O'Connor understood that this is one hard fact humankind would rather ignore, and her characters show extraordinary initiative and ingenuity in finding ways to avoid confronting their frailties, the chief of

Taken from *Flannery O'Connor: A Proper Scaring*, revised edition, by Jill Pelaez Baumgaertner. Copyright © 1999 by Jill Pelaez Baumgaertner. Published by Cornerstone Press, Chicago, 1999. Reprinted with permission.

which is their own mortality. It is often only when a character smacks flat up against death that the necessity of salvation is finally apparent. That is why so many of O'Connor's stories reach a violent climax, forcing the characters to see grace in a new and terrible way.

THE EMBLEMATIC MOMENT

Sight and insight are intimately connected metaphors in O'Connor's stories—for both character and reader. Josephine Hendin has adopted the phrase "comic literalization" to describe the metaphorical development in these works. "Beginning with a metaphoric statement," she writes, "the story develops as the metaphor becomes realized in a concrete action or material object." At key moments—often at the height of a story's crisis, sometimes at a moment of foreshadowing— O'Connor clicks the camera and catches a strange picture. In the seventeenth century, these would have been called emblems; and the fictive moment containing them, the emblematic moment. In her stories she adds a further dimension to these moments, transforming them into spiritual epiphanies.

For the seventeenth-century reader emblems were the pictorial representations of scriptural truth—highly exaggerated yet literal. Emblems literalized a motto, epigram, or scriptural passage to provoke a new response to an old and often too familiar saying. Thus, the picture used in Francis Quarles's emblem book, *Emblems, Divine and Moral* (1635) to illustrate the verse, "Stay my steps in thy paths that my feet do not slide" (Psalm 17:5) shows a person in a child's walker being led through the streets by an angel. The steps are literally "stayed." The feet do not slide because the walker supports and the angel guides.

HOW O'CONNOR'S EMBLEMS WORK

O'Connor's emblems work in similar ways. She often paints stark pictures which draw attention to themselves both pictorially, as still moments caught in time, and emblematically, as exaggerated representations of deeper spiritual truths. In "The Geranium" the flower pot crashes to the pavement, and the flowers lie on the ground, roots in the air. The camera clicks. In "The Barber" Rayber runs out of the barber shop, his bib still on, lather dripping from his chin. The camera clicks again. In "Revelation" Mrs. Turpin, leaning on the fence, turns the water on the hogs. In "Parker's

Back" Parker leaves his shoes burning in the middle of the field. In each of O'Connor's stories, the climactic moment could be lifted from a seventeenth-century emblem book. These moments are often violent, bizarre, surprising. The Christ tattooed on Parker's back is beaten with a broom. The old lady whose family has just been shot reaches in sudden affection for her killer. The child drowns in the river in which he has been baptized.

O'Connor always pushes us back to the agonizing scandal of the cross. That scandal has at its heart the recognition that humanity is fallen and needs redemption. Of course, for the Christian the mysteries remain mysterious to the end.

Toward the end of O'Connor's letters, one experiences a depressing sense of inevitability. As one approaches August 3, 1964, the temptation is simply to stop reading—as if that would somehow keep O'Connor alive. Sally Fitzgerald notes that O'Connor's final letter, written on July 29th, 1964, and found on her nightstand after her death, is almost illegible. It is playful in its nicknaming, but serious in its brief contents, and refers to an anonymous phone call her friend received. "Be properly scared," O'Connor advises, "and go on doing what you have to do, but take the necessary precautions. . . . Cheers, Tarfunk."

Such proper scaring is what many of O'Connor's characters and all of her readers require and experience in her fiction. We must go on doing what we have to do, but with clearer eyes and more sensitive ears, having run into Truth along the way.

O'Connor's Bleak View of Human Nature

Martha Stephens

The prevalence of devastation, annihilation, and ugliness in O'Connor's work has led some critics to determine that her view of the world—and the people inhabiting it—was overwhelmingly negative. In the selection that follows, Martha Stephens contends that O'Connor's fiction is made oppressive by her stubborn refusal to see any goodness, beauty, dignity, or meaning in ordinary human life. According to Stephens, O'Connor's contempt for human nature is evidenced by the grotesque imagery she uses to describe her characters. A professor of modern literature and creative writing at the University of Cincinnati, Stephens is the author of *The Question of Flannery O'Connor*, from which this article is excerpted, and two novels set in South Georgia.

Flannery O'Connor is not likely to prove, in the long run, an easy writer to assess; and it may well be that many a future chronicler of American letters, poised on the edge of an O'Connor judgment, will find himself much vexed. . . .

That she was a gifted writer—astonishingly good at times—certainly no one wishes to dispute; but the fact is that she was possessed of so eccentric, at times so—we must face this to begin with—repugnant a view of human life that the strain of trying to enter emotionally into her work is often very great indeed. No one was more conscious of this problem than she herself; she was very much aware of facing an audience essentially hostile to her assumptions about human life, and she did not expect—nor, one sometimes thinks, did she even desire—easy acceptance from it. She said that what she wanted to do was to restore the reader's "sense of evil," and she obviously did not expect that he would wholly enjoy it.

Reprinted by permission of Louisiana State University Press from *The Question of Flannery O'Connor*, by Martha Stephens. Copyright © 1973 by Louisiana State University Press.

A HIGHLY DOCTRINAL WRITER

The problem, then, in trying to make a balanced judgment about this writer is simple enough to state. O'Connor clearly had a great natural gift for the story-telling art—the better one knows her work, the more one comes to respect her ability. But she was also a highly doctrinal writer with a marked evangelical strain, and like all such writers—like D. H. Lawrence, for instance, and in France her fellow Catholics François Mauriac and Georges Bernanos—she poses so personal, so goading a challenge to a reader's perceptions of life that coming to terms with her as an artist is difficult.

To say that Miss O'Connor was a devout Catholic hardly begins to suggest how formidable the distance is between her view of life and the prevailing view of modern readers. To find so bleak, so austere and rigid, so other-worldly a Christian view of life as hers, one is forced back into the distant past of English religious literature—into the dark side of medieval Christian thought with its constant injunction to renunciation of the world. "All Christen people, biholde and see/ This world is but a vanytee"—her stories, like the twelfth-century verse, seem to enjoin us. How can it be, the O'Connor books seem to ask, that—in the words this time of the *Everyman* poet—"every man liveth so after their own pleasure and yet of their life they be nothing sure"? Let us beware, they urge, that it is not with us as it was with the evil ones in the time of Lot, for they too—in the words of Saint Luke—"did eat, they drank, they bought, they sold, they planted, they builded; But the same day that Lot went out of Sodom it rained fire and brimstone from heaven, and destroyed them all."

One must, of course, say *seem*—the stories *seem* to enjoin, to ask, to urge, for one does not wish to imply that the O'Connor stories and novels are not wholly dramatic. On the contrary, there is not a word of authorial argument as such. And yet the message and the warning are there; in story after story O'Connor sets up her Sodom and brings it down, sets it up and brings it down. Here the wretched Mrs. Mays, the Mrs. Copes, the Raybers and Julians and Asburys suffer their terrible Christian comeuppance—foolish, deluded creatures who think they possess something, know something, can achieve something, who (as if, like brute animals, they have never discovered the fact of their own mortality) take some dumb pride in having reached a position of material or emotional security. "I've seen them come, and I've seen them go," says Mrs. McIntyre of her hired help, and we know she's thinking, "But I'm here, I stay, I'm safe." But of course no one is safe; eventually the fire and brimstone is rained down—O'Connor brings on, to wreak their destruction, her mad bulls, her demonic children, her escaped convicts. See, these stories seem to say, devastation, annihilation always around the corner, and yet the godless go on acting as if they held their fates in their own hands. . . .

O'CONNOR'S CONTEMPT FOR ORDINARY HUMAN LIFE

What is oppressive about the O'Connor work as a whole, what is sometimes intolerable, is her stubborn refusal to see any good, any beauty or dignity or meaning, in ordinary human life on earth. A good indication of what must be called O'Connor's contempt for ordinary human life is the loathing with which she apparently contemplated the human body. She liked to describe faces—she hardly ever passed up an opportunity—and nearly all her faces are ugly. In the first novel, *Wise Blood*, this seems to be true without exception; human faces remind her of rodents, cats, hogs, mandrills, and vegetables; they are frog-like, hawk-like, gap-toothed, mildewed, shale-textured, red-skinned, stupid, demented, and simply "evil." Each part of the physiognomy comes in for its share of abuse; hair is likened to dirty mops and rings of sausages—it is said to stream down the face like ham gravy. One could continue the catalog—but the point, I think, is clear. Human beings are ugly in every way; the human form itself is distinctly unpleasant to behold; human life is a sordid, almost unrelievedly hideous affair. The only human act that is worthy of respect is the act of renouncing all worldly involvement, pleasure, and achievement.

Now, about the short stories, it is quite true that if we take the O'Connor stories individually they seem in this respect much less oppressive; but reading them back to back by volume—one of the ways, surely, that we expect to be able to read short stories—one may find his resistance mounting to the view of life that together they present. We may well grant that here is Mrs. May, comically self-adoring and self-righteous in spite of the fact that, as all can plainly see, she is a narrow-minded, deluded, ridiculous old fool; here is Asbury, a failed artist—contemptibly convinced of his total superiority over everyone else and yet childishly blaming his failures on his mother; here are poor old Mrs. Cope, Mrs. Turpin (who thanks God for good disposition), the appalling Ruby Hill. The images of these people rise up so graphically before us as we read—their manners, their speech are so cunningly done—that we freely respond to their reality within the story. Yet at the same time, one is dimly aware that the author is trying to make their stories say something, prove something about life, to which one cannot respond. For the revelation that O'Connor wanted to push us to—the truth about life that she wanted to force us to grant—was that these people represent, even at their comic worst, the norm of modern society.

And one's own experience simply will not support such a view. With all one's admiration for the high technical brilliance of O'Connor's work, for her cunning selection of detail and delicate sense for nuance in speech and manners, and for the wonderfully controlled momentum with which her stories move—even with all this, one's pleasure is at least diminished by the fact that what the stories are moving *to* is a truth or hypothesis about life that sometimes seems hardly worth our consideration. We may feel that the stories would appear, seen from a certain point of view, nearly perfectly executed, but that that point of view is not ours, that—to restate the dilemma in Boothian terms—we cannot be the readers the stories require us to be.

O'Connor's Place in the Literary Tradition of the South

C. Hugh Holman

As a writer living in the American South, Flannery O'Connor is often associated with a literary tradition that includes William Faulkner, Carson McCullers, Truman Capote, and Tennessee Williams. C. Hugh Holman maintains that, like other eminent Southern writers, O'Connor was fascinated with the grotesque elements of the South; furthermore, she was sympathetic to the views of the Southern Agrarians, a literary group that sought to preserve the distinctive, non-industrial character of the South. However, contends Holman, the crucial difference between O'Connor and other Southern writers lies in her devotion to Christianity and its tenets. Holman is the author of several books of literary criticism.

Nathaniel Hawthorne once stated his intention "to achieve a novel that should evolve some deep lesson and should possess physical substance enough to stand alone." He was describing the ambition of many writers of fiction, but his remark is peculiarly appropriate to the work of Flannery O'Connor, a brilliantly gifted writer whose death at the age of thirty-nine silenced one of the finest voices of American fiction. Hawthorne's statement is particularly useful in looking at Miss O'Connor's work because of his separation—or at least his distinction—between meaning and matter, a distinction often overlooked by the numerous reviewers who have seen Flannery O'Connor as simply another writer of Southern Gothic and have easily grouped her with other Southern writers of the grotesque such as Erskine Caldwell, Carson McCullers, Truman Capote, and Tennessee Williams. Indeed, Caroline Gordon once derisively quoted

Excerpted from "Her Rue with a Difference: Flannery O'Connor and the Southern Literary Tradition," by C. Hugh Holman in *The Added Dimension: The Art and Mind of Flannery O'Connor*, edited by Melvin J. Friedman and Lewis A. Lawson. Copyright © 1966, 1977 by Fordham University Press. Reprinted with permission.

the assertion of a critic that "if the name of the author were deleted it would be hard to tell a story by Miss O'Connor from a story by Truman Capote, Carson McCullers or Tennessee Williams."

However wrong that critic was, there certainly can be little question that Miss O'Connor was a Southern writer. The South, particularly that of piedmont Georgia and eastern Tennessee, is what she called her "country." "The country that the writer is concerned with in the most objective way is," she said, ". . . the region that most immediately surrounds him, or simply the country, with its body of manners, that he knows well enough to employ." Out of this South and its people she quarried the "physical substance" which gave her work the living elements of successful fiction.

PART OF A SOUTHERN LITERARY TRADITION

But, as has been obvious to all but the most unperceptive of her critics, this "physical substance" for her was not an end in itself; she hungered passionately for meaning and worked hard to "evolve" from her country "Some deep lesson." Here, too, she was a part of a "Southern literary tradition." For if she seemed in immediate subject matter to belong to the "school of the Southern Gothic," she seemed also to find in the Southern experience a lesson for the present, as did the Agrarians, or a cosmic truth, as did the apocalyptic mythologizers like Faulkner. Such association with any Southern "school," whether it be Agrarian or that preoccupied, as she said, "with everything deformed and grotesque," irritated her. She declared, "The woods are full of regional writers, and it is the great horror of every serious Southern writer that he will become one of them." I not only sympathize with her attitude; I also find her relation to the Southern literary tradition to be unusual and illuminating both about her and about the tradition itself. Indeed, in looking at her native Georgia, like many modern Southerners, Miss O'Connor's vision was touched with rue, but she wore her "rue with a difference"—a difference that helps to define her essential quality and to give us a deeper insight into her "country," both of soil and spirit.

Geographically, hers was a special South, remote from the moss-draped melancholy great oaks and the stable social order of the Atlantic seaboard and equally distant from the tropical lushness and fecundity of the gulf-coast Deep

South. She knew and wrote of piedmont Georgia and eastern Tennessee—a rolling, sparsely wooded land where both the spring freshets and the ravishing plow pierce its surface to leave gaping wounds of dark red clay. It is cotton country, made up of small farms, small towns, and widely-spaced small cities—a country at the mercy of capricious weather and the vicissitudes of the cotton market, which has been in a fluctuating state but one that has always remained depressed since the 1920s. It is a land wracked by diseases peculiar to poverty, by a vicious sharecropper system, by little education, and a superstitious, intense, pietistic but non-theological religious passion. Hers is not the South of the Virginia Tidewater or the Carolina low-country, regions that are nominally Episcopal in religion, aristocratic in dream if not in fact, and tied to a past culture that reverenced learning, practiced law, and dreamed of a republican government of merit founded upon the doctrines of the eighteenth-century enlightenment.

Miss O'Connor's segment of the South was settled, in large measure, by the Scotch-Irish who came down the inland cattle trails from Pennsylvania. By 1790 the Scotch-Irish represented over a quarter of a million Americans. They had entered principally through the ports of Philadelphia, Chester, or New Castle, and had followed the Great Valley westward for about a hundred miles, until tall mountains blocked their trail. Then they had turned south into Virginia, the Carolinas, Tennessee, and Georgia. They were a poverty-stricken, harsh, impetuous people, with a deep sense of integrity, a tendency to make their own laws, and to worship God with individual and singular fervor. Once in the Southern piedmont, they fanned out to encompass the region, and to help define its qualities, among whose most noticeable characteristics was a widespread social crudity marked, as even the sympathetic historians of the Scotch-Irish point out, by brutal fights, animal cruelty, and folk hilarity. The journal of the Anglican Reverend Charles Woodmason is a graphic account of the shocking effect which this primitive life made upon a Tidewater minister who visited it and saw its chief characteristics as lawlessness, vile manners, ignorance, slovenliness, and primitive emotionalism in religion. These people's pragmatic frugality, their oversimplified—almost folk-version—Calvinistic religion, and their intense individualism formed a distinct but not always attractive culture. Here, in the foothills near the early rises of the mountains, the Scotch-Irish were joined by the refugees and malcontents of the established seaboard society to form a harsh and unmannered world. . . .

O'CONNOR'S REPRESENTATION OF THE GROTESQUE

It is with these piedmont people whose literary representation has always been as grotesques that Miss O'Connor deals; they constitute the "physical substance" out of which she fashioned her vision of reality. In our time much these same groups of Southerners have been the subject matter of Erskine Caldwell, Carson McCullers, and the Southern Gothic School in general.

The representation of the grotesque is a characteristic of much twentieth-century writing, Southern and otherwise. In a fruitful and provocative essay on "The Grotesque: An American Genre," William Van O'Connor, who includes Miss O'Connor among the writers he discusses, states that the representation of an inverted world in which "what most of us would take to be normal is presented as monstrous" results from the fact that "the old agricultural system depleted the land and poverty breeds abnormality; in many cases people were living with a code that was no longer applicable, and this meant a detachment from reality and loss of vitality." Although he sees "clear antecedents" in Edgar Allan Poe and finds the genre practiced by Caldwell, Faulkner, Robert Penn Warren, Eudora Welty, Carson McCullers, and Tennessee Williams, all of whom certainly use Southern grotesques, his emphasis on a decayed order and lost wealth, an emphasis pertinent to many Southern writers, does not seem to apply very well to Miss O'Connor's works.

He comes much closer to her position when he quotes Thomas Mann on the grotesque as resulting from the fact that modern art "has ceased to recognize the categories of tragic and comic. . . . It sees life as tragi-comedy, with the result that the grotesque is its most genuine style . . . the only guise in which the sublime may appear." Miss O'Connor seemed to have the same view of the grotesque. In a preface written in 1962 for a reprinting of *Wise Blood* she said, "It is a comic novel about a Christian *malgré lui,* and as such, very serious, for all comic novels that are any good must be about matters of life and death." For, while there is no question that Flannery O'Connor deals with Southern characters who

THE UNIQUE QUALITY OF SOUTHERN WRITING
In the selection that follows, excerpted from a speech entitled "The Regional Writer," O'Connor explains why there are so many good Southern writers.

The best American fiction has always been regional. The ascendancy passed roughly from New England to the Midwest to the South; it has passed to and stayed longest wherever there has been a shared past, a sense of alikeness, and the possibility of reading a small history in a universal light. In these things the South still has a degree of advantage. . . .

Every serious writer will put his finger on it at a slightly different spot but in the same region of sensitivity. When Walker Percy won the National Book Award, newsmen asked him why there were so many good Southern writers and he said, "Because we lost the War." He didn't mean that simply that a lost war makes good subject matter. What he was saying was that we have had our Fall. We have gone into the modern world with an inburnt knowledge of human limitations and with a sense of mystery which could not have developed in our first state of innocence—as it has not sufficiently developed in the rest of our country.

Flannery O'Connor, *Mystery and Manners*. New York: Farrar, Straus & Giroux, 1969.

are grotesques, the grotesque element in her work has other sources than the heat of social anger which warms Erskine Caldwell's or the sense of the absurdity of human existence which shapes the grotesqueries of our young existentialists.

SUPPORTING A SOUTHERN WAY OF LIFE

She is more nearly central to the Southern literary tradition in her persistent passion for order. Confronted with a modern, mechanized, scientifically-oriented world, the leading literary spokesmen for the South have usually shared the discomfort that most producers of humane art experience in the presence of the mechanical, and, like the twelve at Vanderbilt in 1930, they "tend to support a Southern way of life against what may be called the American or prevailing way." Almost all artists feel a hunger for meaning, a need for structure, and rage for order in existence, and believe that the human spirit should never calmly surrender its endless search for order. Twentieth-century writers confronted by the spectacle of the mechanized culture of America have taken many different roads to many different regions of the spirit. Some have sought in art itself a kind of solipsistic answer to the need of order and thus have made a religion of art. Some have sought in activist movements bent on social change a way to establish meaning in the world. The Southerner, predisposed to look backward as a result of his concern with the past, has tended to impose a desire for a social structure that reflects moral principles and he has tried to see in the past of his region at least the shadowy outlines of a viable and admirable moral-social world. Allen Tate, in 1952, in a retrospective glance at the Agrarian movement said:

> I never thought of Agrarianism as a *restoration* of anything in the Old South; I saw it as something to be created, as I think it will in the long run be created as the result of a profound change, not only in the South, but elsewhere, in the moral and religious outlook of western man. . . . What I had in mind twenty years ago . . . presupposes, with us, a prior order, the order of a unified Christendom. The Old South perpetuated many of the virtues of such an order; but to try to "revive" the Old South, and to build a wall around it, would be a kind of idolatry; it would prefer the accident to the substance. If there is a useful program that we might undertake in the South, would it not be towards the greater unity of the varieties of Southern Protestantism, with the ultimate aim the full unity of all Christians? We are told by our Northern friends that the greatest menace to the South is ignorance; but there is even greater ignorance of the delusion of progressive enlightenment.

Miss O'Connor was generally in sympathy with such views of the Agrarians. When she makes statements such as this one from "The Fiction Writer and His Country" she seems almost to be echoing their beliefs: "The anguish that most of us have observed for some time now has been caused not by the fact that the South is alienated from the rest of the country, but by the fact that it is not alienated enough, that every day we are getting more and more like the rest of the country, that we are being forced out, not only of our many sins but of our few virtues." And certainly one could hardly call a friend of science the creator of Hulga Hopewell, in "Good Country People," who has a Ph.D. in philosophy, a wooden leg, and a willingness to be seduced by a fake Bible salesman who steals the leg and leaves her betrayed and helpless in the hay loft. Hulga underlines this statement in one of the books that she endlessly reads and marks up:

> Science, on the other hand, has to assert its soberness and seriousness afresh and declare that it is concerned solely with

what-is. Nothing—how can it be for science anything but a horror and a phantasm? If science is right, then one thing stands firm: science wishes to know nothing of nothing. Such is after all the strictly scientific approach to Nothing. We know it by wishing to know nothing of Nothing.

The girl, like others of Miss O'Connor's few intellectuals, declares to the Bible salesman, "We are all damned . . . but some of us have taken off our blindfolds and see that there's nothing to see. It's a kind of salvation." Similarly Rayber, in *The Violent Bear It Away*, with all his knowledge seems to be rendered more helpless by all he learns, and falls the semi-credulous victim of a lustful child who is not really a spokesman for love but simply for the power of emotion.

"The Displaced Person," a short story that recounts the intrusion into a widow's farm of an efficient and effective displaced person, is typical of the way in which Miss O'Connor's situations can be read in frames not unlike those of the Agrarians. Here the "displaced person" may be taken as symbolic of the mechanical world intruding itself from the outside to disrupt the "order" of a Southern farm. Read this way the story is not unlike Robert Penn Warren's "The Patented Gate and the Mean Hamburger," and yet a careful examination of Miss O'Connor's tone and action makes one, I think, suspicious of such a reading, a suspicion confirmed for the reader by the fact that Mrs. McIntyre, the widow who owns the farm, rejects its chance of salvation by Mr. Guizac, effectively destroys him, and declares to Father Flynn, who has been his friend and advocate, "As far as I'm concerned . . . Christ was just another D.P."

O'CONNOR'S SOUTHERN CONCERNS

Flannery O'Connor's work is sufficiently similar to that of her contemporaries in the South to justify our feeling that, in one sense at least, she shares not only a common subject but many common concerns. She has other characteristics in common with her Southern contemporaries that are worth mentioning. For her, as for them—and, indeed, for any depicter of an agrarian culture—the social unit is the family. For her, as it seemingly did for Faulkner and Wolfe, concrete expressions of meaning seem to come in relatively small actions and limited scenes. Wolfe is most impressive as an artist in his short stories and short novels, and much of Faulkner's best work appeared in brief episodes which were later woven into novels. Miss O'Connor, too, is better as a writer of short stories than she is as a novelist. To examine, for example, *Wise Blood* as a novel after looking at the original appearance of some of its parts as short stories is to question to some degree her wisdom in attempting the larger organization.

She also has an awareness of the caste structures that a relatively fixed social order produces and which have fascinated many Southern writers, even though she does not often write of any except her "poor whites." For example, in her story "Revelation," she says:

> Sometimes Mrs. Turpin occupied herself at night naming the classes of people. On the bottom of the heap were most colored people, not the kind she would have been if she had been one, but most of them; then next to them—not above, just away from—were the white-trash; then above them were the homeowners, and above them the home-and-land owners, to which she and Claud belonged. Above she and Claud were people with a lot of money and much bigger houses and much more land. But here the complexity of it would begin to bear in on her, for some of the people with a lot of money were common and ought to be below she and Claud and some of the people who had good blood had lost their money and had to rent and then there were colored people who owned their homes and land as well. There was a colored dentist in town who had two red Lincolns and a swimming pool and a farm with registered white-face cattle on it.

Miss O'Connor's sense that this kind of class distinction is meaningless is made plain here, and such things seem finally to be of much less interest to her than they are to most Southern writers.

But these, after all, are largely quibbles. The crucial similarities and differences lie elsewhere. They lie with the concern she has for a religious order, and her most significant differences with her Southern contemporaries are in the same area.

THE CRUCIAL DIFFERENCE BETWEEN O'CONNOR AND OTHER SOUTHERNERS

The crucial difference between Miss O'Connor and most of her fellow Southerners lies in a simple fact, which she seldom passed up an opportunity to emphasize. She was a Catholic novelist in the Protestant South. Indeed, she speaks of the writing of fiction in terms of religious vocation, and she declares, "I see from the standpoint of Christian orthodoxy. This means that for me the meaning of life is centered in our Redemption by Christ and that what I see in the world I see in its relation to that." Hence the order she sees in the world, the order which redeems it from chaos and gives it community, is fundamentally religious. And the tragedy she sees is the failure of the seeking soul to find rest in an adequate God. . . .

"Our souls," St. Augustine said, "are restless till they find rest in Thee." Flannery O'Connor's restless souls belong to people primitive in mind and Protestant in religion, who with all their difference, share a common, deep, and personal awareness of the awful and awesome presence and power of God in the world. Like Francis Thompson in "The Hound of Heaven" no matter how much they flee "Him down the labyrinthine ways," they cannot deny either His reality or His intolerable demands. Living in a world not ordered to an adequate sense of the power and presence of God, they seek either to deny Him or to pervert Him, and thus they become grotesque and unnatural. The human hunger for love cannot be satisfied with hatred; the human passion for order cannot willingly accept disorder as the principle of its universe; the ultimate dignity of man does not lie in his own hands, and when he tries to take violent hold of it, he destroys himself. That, it seems to me, is the anti-existentialist message that a brave and thoughtful Catholic woman gave to a South hungry, as it has been for a century and a half, for a stable order and a sensible meaning. Because she was Southern, she used the South as matter and addressed it as audience. But what she said transcends her region and speaks with the authority of art to the great world outside.

Representations of Race in O'Connor's Work

Ralph C. Wood

Flannery O'Connor's personal correspondence, in which she makes negative remarks about blacks, has led many critics to conclude that she was a racist. However, as Ralph C. Wood argues in the subsequent article, representations of race in O'Connor's fiction suggest the opposite conclusion. Wood contends that in her favorite story, "The Artificial Nigger," O'Connor transforms a racist symbol of the South into an emblem of antiracist redemption. Wood, a professor of theology and literature at Baylor University in Waco, Texas, is the author of a number of books about religion in literature, including *The Comedy of Redemption: Christian Faith and Comic Vision in Four American Novelists*, and also serves as the editor-at-large for *Christian Century* magazine.

Flannery O'Connor's art makes powerful testimony to the profoundest commonalities shared by blacks and whites, chiefly our common dependence on the grace and judgment of God. But O'Connor's recently revealed correspondence with her friend Maryat Lee will surely lead many to conclude that the novelist was a racist. In the letters O'Connor not only makes unsavory remarks about blacks; she also reveals herself to have been deeply out of sympathy with the civil rights crusade of the 1960s. Both disclosures threaten to undermine our esteem for the most important southern writer since Faulkner.

The time has come to assess the question of racism in O'Connor's work. It is especially important to do so because she was, first and last, an avowed and unapologetic Christian. She declared herself to be "no vague believer." She was a Catholic, she said, "not like someone else would be a Baptist or a Methodist but like someone else would be an atheist." O'Connor confessed her work to be rooted in "the central Christian mystery: that [the world] has, for all its horror, been found by God to be worth dying for." Everything she saw and said and wrote sprang from this central belief. What, then, does it mean if this writer was also racist at heart?

We need to assess O'Connor's racial attitudes also in order to take the measure of our own. The word "racism" is often used to silence debate. We can dismiss those who disagree with us on race issues by deploying the "racist" epithet. It need not be so, for the term has specifiable meaning: a racist is someone who denies the dignity and worth of other human beings because of their skin color, asserts the inherent superiority of one's own race over all others, and thus mistreats members of the so-called inferior races. Politically, racism means a refusal of the justice and the equality of opportunity that are due to every citizen of a republic whose Constitution is colorblind. Theologically, racism rejects the doctrine that all people are created in the image of God, that all races have sinned and fallen short of God's glory, that we are therefore brothers and sisters saved not by our own righteousness but by the death and resurrection of Jesus Christ. Neither politically nor theologically, I will argue, was O'Connor a racist. On the contrary, she was a writer who, though not without temptation and struggle, offers the real antidote to racism. . . .

NEW SINS COMMITTED TO CORRECT ANCIENT EVILS

In "Everything That Rises Must Converge" O'Connor prophesied against the new sins that were being committed in the attempt to correct ancient evils. The story concerns a frustrated young college graduate named Julian who still lives at home with his mother. He becomes obsessed with a desire to expose and reform his mother's racial sins. In willful defiance of her segregationist attitudes, and in attempted solidarity with a victim of racial injustice, Julian sits down by a black man on a bus. The Negro instantly penetrates the self-seeking dimension in such white "charity," brusquely refusing Julian's attempt to use him as the means for practicing his own moral hygiene.

Julian's mother could have taken advantage of her son's public humiliation, but she does not. Though conventionally prejudiced, Julian's mother is capable of the love that matters most: she cares deeply about her uncaring son. And despite her verbal scorn for blacks, she is no vicious racist. On the contrary, she humorously accepts the hard lesson in economic equality that she is forced to learn: across the aisle is a black woman wearing a purple hat identical to her own. This humbling revelation does not sour her friendly and outgoing nature. Indeed, she remains so jovial and affectionate that a little black boy—whose mother wears the selfsame hat—is instinctively drawn to her. Julian's mother innocently plays peek-a-boo with the child and then gives him a penny as they get off the bus.

The black mother is infuriated. Blinded by a racial rage that makes her unable to distinguish a kindly from a condescending gesture, she lashes out in murderous fury, striking Julian's mother to the ground and giving her a fatal stroke. Yet even as she dies, the white lady remains gracious.

In her addled state of mind, she calls out for Caroline, the black nurse from her childhood. Yet the real murderer is not the black woman but Julian himself. He has been so obsessed with casting out the racist mote in his mother's eye that he remains oblivious to the beamlike presumption and ingratitude that afflict his own vision. Julian can "love" the anonymous Negro whom he does not know, but not the mother whom he does know and who also knows him.

O'Connor surprisingly reveals, therefore, that the voice crying with hatred and the hand striking with death spring not only from the seething envy of rednecks but also from the unredeemed rage of the righteous, black or white. Yet such human evil cannot finally block the workings of divine mercy—the burning mercy, as O'Connor called it, that incinerates sin. His mother's death prompts Julian to a searing moment of self-recognition. He sees that her conventional racism has blinded him to her unconventional graciousness. Having discerned it at last, Julian embarks for his true country, "the world of guilt and sorrow."

. . . O'Connor was cool toward the civil rights movement [because] she feared its advocates lacked a proper regard for the time and patience required to embody social justice. There is an old southern saying: "In the North they don't care how high blacks rise, so long as they don't get too close.

In the South, we don't care how close blacks get, so long as they don't rise too high." O'Connor knew that the integration of southern society would complicate interracial closeness with interracial competition. Blacks who already lived near at hand would begin to compete economically and educationally with whites, especially poor whites. To make racial equality work socially no less than legally would be a matter of civil manners rather than civil rights. "For the rest of the country," she observed, "the race problem is settled when the Negro has his rights, but for the southerner, whether he's white or colored, that's only the beginning."

A NEW CODE OF MANNERS

O'Connor called for a new code of manners to help ensure mutual regard rather than internecine hatred. It may seem exceedingly odd, even antique, to speak of manners at this late date in our history, especially knowing how the old southern manners often reinforced racist conventions. But for O'Connor, manners were the indispensable means for enacting the social roles without which we would not be selves at all. Even in their negative form, they ensure the necessary social distance which our sinfulness requires, protecting us against heedlessly intruding into others' privacy. At their best, manners maintain civility and cordiality among people who may feel an instinctive antipathy. They enable us to treat others with respect even when we don't like them. "Formality preserves that individual privacy which everybody needs and, in these times, is always in danger of losing."

To grant blacks their civil rights without working out a new interracial decorum—a new code of formality that preserves privacy—would drive out the devil of injustice, only to welcome in seven new devils of incivility. O'Connor forecast our present situation: justice without civility and courtesy leads to enforced codes of speech and behavior that are as oppressive as the injustice they seek to correct.

What is most lamentably lost is the greatest requisite of all: the sense of humor. We will have achieved racial sanity, I believe, when blacks and whites can joke together about our apprehensions and misapprehensions. Most of O'Connor's blacks possess this gift of laughter that eases pain. They have survived their suffering, in very large part, through their comically mannered means for fending off evil. "The uneducated southern Negro is not the clown he's made out to be," O'Connor observed. "He's a man of very elaborate manners and great formality which he uses superbly for his own protection and to insure his own privacy."

Perhaps the chief item in the repertoire of black manners is the art of "signifying": the verbal device for taunting oppressive whites with false praise. What often appears as "Tomming"—abject acquiescence to the whites—can be used to get revenge by indirection, to save oneself from returning evil for evil, and thus to preserve one's own sense of dignity and worth when the white world has denied it. O'Connor had an especially keen ear for this black gift.

In "The Enduring Chill," two Negro workers named Randall and Morgan play a wicked trick on Asbury Fox, the white intellectual who wants to liberate them from his mother's seemingly repressive rules for running her dairy. Asbury regards his mother as a rabid racist for refusing to let her black laborers have their fill of the farm's nutritious and abundant milk. Yet the uneducated Randall and Morgan prove far smarter than the cultured Asbury: they know that to drink unpasteurized milk is to court disease.

They also see that Asbury's professed solidarity with them is a form of moral preening. So little does Asbury know Randall and Morgan that he cannot tell them apart. Yet he wants them to imbibe the forbidden milk with him in a secular communion that would defy his mother's racist restrictions. After encouraging the gullible Asbury to drink deeply of this sickening font, the two black men offer their own devastating commentary:

> "Howcome you let him drink that milk every day?"

> "What he do is him," Randall said. "What I do is me."

> "Howcome he talks so ugly about his ma?"

> "Because she ain't whup him enough when was little," Randall said.

Asbury earns the wages of his sinful righteousness when he contracts undulant fever. Though he hopes to die as a martyr to his mother's villainy, his disease is not, alas, fatal. Yet even as he lies sick, Asbury seeks to spite his mother in an act of forced friendship with the two black workers. Randall and Morgan will have nothing of it. When Asbury offers them a cigarette in yet another gesture of spurious commonality, Randall seizes the whole pack. The two Negroes take their leave of the undying Asbury only after indulging in a final session of "signifying."

"You certly does look well."

"I'm about to die," Asbury said irritably.

"You looks fine," Randall said.

"You be up and around in a few days," Morgan predicted.

Manners may provide comic relief from injustice and self-righteousness. They may even ensure an essential respect among people who are divided by preference and experience. But manners remain fundamentally dependent on an underlying charity. Manners have no power to transform human existence, to engender new life, to reconcile those who have sinned against each other. Our proverbial southern sweetness has often served to mask horrible evils: we have killed with our kindness no less than our meanness.

O'Connor seems not to have discerned these limits. Though she was a writer who declared that her stories are so violent because her characters have such hard heads, she failed to see that firm federal intervention was required for the South—indeed, for the nation—to overcome racial injustice. Nor did she discern that lesser incivilities may have to be tolerated in order that greater barbarities—both the subtle and the egregious acts of racist terrorism to which blacks were often subjected—might be ended.

The Miracle of Racial Reconciliation

But about the deepest racial ratter O'Connor remained clear. She understood that, severed from charity, both morals and manners are without foundation. Nothing less and nothing other than the grace of God can work the miracle that enables the races not merely to tolerate each other but to live together as redeemed and reconciled brothers and sisters of the same Lord.

O'Connor reveals the nature of such a miracle in her favorite story, "The Artificial Nigger." She was fond of it, I suspect, because it is a work that inverts a racist symbol into an emblem of antiracist redemption. Indeed, at the three chief turning points of the story, the protagonists are offered redemption by Negroes.

Yet the story is not a study in black and white relations. The characters who stand most drastically in need of reconciliation are divided not by race but by will. A grandfather named Mr. Head and his grandson named Nelson dwell alone in the remoteness of rural Georgia. Though they should be bound by the most blessed ties of familial interdependence, they are bitterly determined to dominate each other. These two rustics have never heard of Nietzsche, but their nihilistic will to power lies at the heart of the modern malaise. Only in overcoming the demonic urge to subject others to our desires, O'Connor shows, can there be hope for families or races.

Their first offer of racial redemption occurs on the train to Atlanta. Knowing that Nelson has never seen Negroes, Mr. Head determines to take his grandson to the city in order to teach him the truth about "niggers"—that they are a blackened and unsavory race. No sooner have Nelson and Mr. Head boarded the train than a large coffee-colored Negro strides majestically past them, followed by two young women, as if in a grand procession. One hand resting on his ample stomach, the black man uses the other to pick up and set down his cane in a slow, kingly gait. With his neat mustache and his light-colored suit, with his yellow satin tie and ruby stickpin and sapphire ring, this elderly Negro shows all the signs of prosperity. He has risen well above his assigned state in the segregated South. But having climbed so high, the black man cannot be allowed too close. He is thus walking to the segregated dining car from the black carriage at the rear of the train. Yet there are no marks of resentment in this man who has every right to rage and chafe at his fate. In spite of the injustice done to him, he maintains his quiet but proud dignity.

Once the entourage has passed, Mr. Head does not explain to Nelson that these were Negroes. Instead, hoping to trap the boy in his ignorance, he asks Nelson what he has seen. "A man," Nelson replies. As often happens in O'Connor's fiction, children have an instinctive discernment of the truth. The boy knows what he cannot articulate. Sinfully opaque to such truth, Mr. Head publicly humiliates Nelson for failing to detect "his first nigger." Nelson is furious, of course, but not only at his grandfather for tricking him; he is also enraged at the tan-colored Negro for failing to be recognizably black.

Moralists read this episode as revealing the true nature of racism: it shows how ethnic distinctions are socially constructed, how racial hatred must be willfully inculcated, how we might overcome the petty barriers of race and class and gender by taking our indiscriminate place in the universal human family. O'Connor was no such moralist. She is after something far deeper: she wants to demonstrate why this Negro remains so regally serene despite the discrimination he suffers.

In their sinful struggle for power, grandfather and grandson lose their way in the Dantesque maze of Atlanta's streets, stumbling unawares into the black ghetto. Nelson wants to cry out for help. Gladly would he cast himself upon anyone who could deliver them from their appalling lostness. He is offered such a figure in the presence of a large black woman leaning idly in a doorway. Nelson wants this great Negress to draw him to her huge bosom, to hold him tight in her arms, and to breathe warmly on his face, as he would look "down and down into her eyes."

Though Nelson's longings are vaguely sexual, they are more significantly spiritual and maternal. This white boy would happily collapse in supplication at the feet of this black Madonna. But Nelson can confess his desires neither to the Negro woman nor to Mr. Head. Such a confession would violate the racial code Nelson has so recently and painfully learned. Even worse, it would bring an end to his proud sufficiency. To declare his dependence would open the way to reconciliation with his grandfather. Nelson wants nothing of it. The luxury of alienation is far too rich for either of them to be able to discern in this black woman a sign of their salvation.

Soon Nelson and Mr. Head commit ever more terrible acts of betrayal and spite against each other. So tightly do they entangle themselves in the knot of evil that their plight seems hopeless. In their deepening bewilderment and estrangement, they wander into a white suburb. There they discover "an artificial nigger" in front of an elegant house. This degrading image of black servitude is not carrying a lantern or grasping a horse's reins, but is holding a discolored piece of watermelon. He is supposed to be a smiling and carefree "darky," but he has a chipped eye and he lurches forward at an awkward angle. "It was not possible," declares the narrator, "to tell if the artificial Negro were meant to be young or old; he looked too miserable to be either."

AN EMBLEM OF REDEMPTION

At last Nelson and Mr. Head are able to recognize this third black emblem of redemption as they stand strangely transfixed and transformed before the wretched statue. Though meant to signal the triumph of whites over blacks, it becomes a secular crucifix to these mutually sinful kinsmen. Even their southern and Protestant eyes can discern the sign of the cross. "They could both feel it dissolving their differences like an action of mercy."

O'Connor does not show grandfather and grandson instantly transformed. They will have to work out their redemption the hard way, in fear and trembling, but also in the slow and patient way of manners. Their religious experience will have to issue in a more courteous solicitude for each other, and for any Negroes they may meet in the future.

Among all of O'Connor's works, "The Artificial Nigger" was the story, I suspect, that inspired Alice Walker's judgment about her sister writer from Milledgeville:

> Essential O'Connor is not about race at all, which is why it is so refreshing, coming, as it does, out of such a racial culture. If it can be said to be "about" anything, then it is "about" prophets and prophecy, "about" revelation, and "about" the impact of supernatural grace on human beings who don't have a chance of spiritual growth without it.

I also suspect that the reason O'Connor liked this story best was that it fictionally incarnates her firmest convictions about both race and religion. She instructs herself no less than her readers in the deep things of the gospel. Perhaps O'Connor knew that her own racial sinfulness had been dissolved in an unbidden gift of artistic mercy. It enabled her to turn a racist icon into an ironic testament to the mystery of charity—a mystery which, though always hidden, is infinitely greater than the mystery of iniquity. This "artificial nigger" not only illumines the evident evils of slavery and discrimination but discloses the subtle grace inherent in suffering that can be redemptively borne because God in Christ has borne it himself. Only as we take such suffering upon ourselves, in acts of civil courtesy and racial generosity, can our unmannered, unjust and discourteous society find its radical remedy.

CHAPTER 2

O'Connor's Predominant Themes

The Role of Grace in O'Connor's Fiction

André Bleikasten

In the following selection, French literary critic André Bleikasten asserts that Flannery O'Connor's stories are primarily concerned with grace, defined in Christian theology as the unmerited love of God toward man. According to Bleikasten, grace comes to O'Connor's characters through acts of sudden violence that incite a terrifying self-revelation and a spiritual rebirth. Bleikasten, a professor at the University of Strasbourg in France, is the author of four books about the work of William Faulkner.

For almost all of O'Connor's characters there is a time for denial and a time for submission, a time for sin and a time for atonement. The passage from one to the other is what she has attempted to describe in her two novels, but . . . she shows relatively little interest in the continuities and intricacies of inner growth. Her heroes do not change gradually; they progress—or regress—in fits and starts, through a series of switches and turnabouts rather than through a slow process of maturation. What engages most deeply O'Connor's imagination—and this, incidentally, may account for her feeling more at home in the short story than in the novel—is not so much time as the sudden encounter of time with the timeless: the decisive moments in a man's existence she would have called moments of grace. "My subject in fiction," O'Connor wrote, "is the action of grace in territory held largely by the devil." Grace plays indeed a major part in her novels as in most of her stories, especially the later ones, and as a religious concept it forms the very core of her implicit theology. Left to his own devices, man, as he appears in her fiction, is totally incapable of ensuring his salvation. Whether it degrades itself in grotesque parody or exhausts

Excerpted from "The Heresy of Flannery O'Connor," by André Bleikasten in *Critical Essays on Flannery O'Connor* (Boston: G.K. Hall, 1985) edited by Melvin J. Friedman and Beverly Lyon Clark. Copyright © 1985 by Melvin J. Friedman and Beverly Lyon Clark. Reprinted with permission from The Gale Group.

itself in mad convulsions, his quest for the holy is doomed to derision and failure from the very start. Grace alone saves, and even that is perhaps going too far: reading O'Connor's tales, one rather feels that grace simply makes salvation possible. As for fallen man, he collaborates in his redemption only by default. Instead of grace coming to complete and crown nature—as the mainstream Catholic tradition would have it—it breaks in on it. Bursting like a storm, it strikes with the unpredictable suddenness of a thunderbolt. And paradoxically it is more often than not at the very last moment, at the climax of violence or at the point of death that grace manifests itself, as though these boundary situations were God's supreme snare and the sinner's ultimate chance. It is when Tarwater yields to the temptation of murder and drowns Rayber's son that the hand of God falls upon him, forcing him to baptize the child against his will, and so converting the moment of sin and death into one of rebirth for both murderer and victim. In most of the stories of *Everything That Rises Must Converge,* the flash of grace occurs in similar circumstances, and spiritual conversion is accomplished likewise through a staggering if not annihilating shock. For Mrs. May, the self-righteous widow of "Greenleaf," it is achieved through the fatal encounter with a wild bull; for others it is effected through a son's suicide ("The Lame Shall Enter First") or a mother's death ("Everything That Rises Must Converge"). In the story significantly entitled "Revelation," on the other hand, a seemingly trivial incident is enough to spark off the deep inner commotion that, in O'Connor's fiction, inevitably precedes the moment of supernatural vision: a respectable lady is abused and assaulted by a girl in a doctor's waiting room, and, with her monumental smugness forever shattered, she is eventually granted a vision of heaven in her pig parlor.

THE IMPACT OF GRACE

Grace takes men by surprise. It catches them unawares, stabs them in the back. Nothing heralds the passage from darkness to light. And the light of grace is so sudden and so bright that it burns and blinds before it illuminates. Consider Mrs. May on the verge of death: ". . . she had the look of a person whose sight has been suddenly restored but who finds the light unbearable" ("Greenleaf"). The impact of grace, as evoked by O'Connor, is that of a painful dazzle; it does not flood the soul with joy; her characters experience it as an instantaneous deflagration, a rending and bursting of the whole fabric of their being. For the revelation it brings is first and foremost self-revelation, the terrified recognition of one's nothingness and guilt. As each character is brutally stripped of his delusions, he sees and knows himself at last for what he is: "Asbury blanched and the last film of illusion was torn as if by a whirlwind from his eyes" ("The Enduring Chill"). Not until the soul has reached that ultimate point of searing self-knowledge does salvation become a possibility. Then begins for those who survive the fire of grace, the "enduring" death-in-life of purgatorial suffering: "[Asbury] saw that for the rest of his days, frail, racked, but enduring, he would live in the face of a purifying terror. A feeble cry, a last impossible protest escaped him. But the Holy Ghost, emblazoned in ice instead of fire, continued, implacable, to descend" ("The Enduring Chill"). For Asbury as well as for Julian, grace means "entry into the world of guilt and sorrow" ("Everything That Rises Must Converge"). For others, on the contrary, like Mrs. May or the grandmother of "A Good Man Is Hard to Find," the beginning is quite literally the end, and the price paid for spiritual rebirth is an immediate death.

In O'Connor, grace is not effusion but aggression. It is God's violence responding to Satan's violence, divine counterterror fighting the mutiny of evil. The operations of the divine and of the demonic are so disturbingly alike that the concept of God suggested by her work is in the last resort hardly more reassuring than her Devil. In fairness, one should no doubt allow for the distortions of satire, and be careful to distinguish the God of O'Connor's faith from the God-image of her characters. Her handling of point of view, however, implies no effacement on the part of the narrator, and her dramatic rendering of spiritual issues as well as the imagery she uses to evoke the actions of grace, provide enough clues to what God meant in her imaginative experience.

O'CONNOR'S VISUAL IMAGINATION

O'Connor's imagination is preeminently visual and visionary. Like Conrad's, her art attempts in its own way "to render the highest kind of justice to the visible universe," and far from clouding her perception, her sense of mystery rather adds to its startling clarity and sharpness. It is worth noting too how much of the action of her stories and novels is reflected in the continuous interplay of peeping or peering, prying or spying eyes, and how much importance is accorded throughout to the sheer act of seeing—or not seeing. *Wise Blood* is a prime example: a great deal of its symbolism springs from the dialectic of vision and blindness, and a similar dialectic is also at work in *The Violent Bear It Away* and in many of her stories. For O'Connor seeing is a measure of being: while the sinner gropes in utter darkness, the prophet—in O'Connor's phrase, "a realist of distances"—is above all a seer. In God the faculty of vision is carried to an infinite power of penetration: God is the All-seeing, the absolute Eye, encompassing the whole universe in its eternal gaze.

The cosmic metaphor for the divine eye is the sun. Through one of those reversals of the imagination analyzed by Gaston Bachelard, the sun, in O'Connor's fiction, is not simply the primal source of light that makes all things visible, it is itself capable of vision, it is an eye. In *The Violent Bear It Away* there are few scenes to which the sun is not a benevolent or, more often, malevolent witness. After the old man's death, while Tarwater is reluctantly digging his grave, the sun moves slowly across the sky "circled by a haze of yellow," then becomes "a furious white blister" as he starts listening to the seductive voice of the "stranger." And when he resolves to deny Christian burial to his great-uncle, the sun appears "a furious white, edging its way secretly behind the tops of trees that rose over the hiding place." The sun is likewise a symbol of God's watchful, but this time approving presence in the two parallel scenes where Bishop, the innocent child—rehearsing, as it were, the baptismal rite—jumps into the fountain of a city park:

> The sun, which had been tacking from cloud to cloud, emerged above the fountain. A blinding brightness fell on the lion's tangled marble head and gilded the stream of water rushing from his mouth. Then the light, falling more gently, rested like a hand on the child's white head. His face might have been a mirror where the sun had stopped to watch its reflection.

Almost obtrusive at times in its symbolic emphasis, sun imagery runs throughout the novel. Tarwater's attempted escape from Christ is a flight from God's sun/son, and the failure of the attempt is metaphorically equated with the sun's triumph: on the morning after his baptismal drowning of

Bishop, the "defeated boy" watches the sun rise "majestically with a long red wingspread," and at the close of the novel the victory of its burning light is again proclaimed through Tarwater's "scorched eyes," which look as if "they would never be used for ordinary sights again."

O'Connor's sun is both cosmic eye and heavenly fire. It thus condenses two of her most pregnant symbol patterns in a single image. For fire imagery is indeed as essential in her symbolic language as eye and sight imagery: incandescent suns, flaming skies, burning houses, woods, trees, and bushes—hers is an apocalyptic world forever ablaze. Fire is the visible manifestation of the principle of violence governing the universe, and the ordeal by fire is the *rite de passage* all of O'Connor's heroes are subjected to. A symbol of destruction and death, and a reminder of hell, it is also the favorite instrument of divine wrath and, as the old prophet taught young Tarwater, "even the mercy of the Lord burns." Associated with purification and regeneration as well as evil, fire is the ambiguous sign of the elect and the damned, and its voracity is God's as much as Satan's.

EMBLEMS OF THE SACRED

That eye, sun, and fire are all emblems of the sacred is confirmed by another symbolic figure which both unites and multiplies them in animal form: the peacock. In "The Displaced Person," instead of being associated with human pride and ostentatiousness, the peacock becomes a symbol of the Second Coming, evoking the unearthly splendor of Christ at the Last Judgment. His tail, in O'Connor's description, expands into a cosmic wonder: ". . . his tail hung in front of her, full of fierce planets with *eyes* that were each ringed in green and set against a *sun* that was gold in one second's light and salmon-colored in the next" ("The Displaced Person"; italics added). Later in the same story the peacock reappears, with his ocellated tail gorgeously fanned out against the vastness of the sky: ". . . a gigantic figure stood facing her. It was the color of the *sun* in the early afternoon, white-gold. It was of no definite shape but there were *fiery* wheels with fierce dark *eyes* in them, spinning rapidly all around it" ("The Displaced Person"; italics added).

Immensity, brilliance, splendor, a dizzying profusion of eyes and suns, such are the features O'Connor chooses to celebrate God's power and glory. And one can hardly refrain from the suspicion that power and glory are in her imagination if not in her belief the essential attributes of divinity. In cosmic terms, her God is sun and fire. If one examines her bestiary, one finds birds of prey, cocks, and bulls—animal metaphors which all suggest phallic potency and male aggressiveness. O'Connor's God is Christ the Tiger rather than Christ the Lamb, a God infinitely distant who confronts us with the agonizing mystery of absolute otherness and whose abrupt transcendence is manifested in sudden deflagrations of power. He is the Most High and the Wholly Other. Man's relation to Him is one of vertical tension precluding any form of reciprocity. Small wonder then that the spiritual errancy of O'Connor's heroes turns into a paranoid nightmare: aware of being watched and scrutinized by the relentless eye of the almighty Judge, they are unable ever to see their remote and silent persecutor. Not until grace descends to seize and possess their tormented souls is the infinite distance separating them abolished. Now the celestial Watcher, now a God of prey; first hovering, motionless, above his victim, then swooping with terrible speed to devour it. . . .

O'Connor's version of Christianity is emphatically and exclusively her own. Her fallen world, it is true, is visited by grace, but is grace, as she evokes it in her last stories, anything other than the vertigo of the *nada* and the encounter with death? And who is this God whose very mercy is terror?

Violence in O'Connor's Work

Josephine Hendin

Josephine Hendin is the author of *Vulnerable People: A View of American Fiction Since 1945* and *The World of Flannery O'Connor*, from which this article is selected. In it, Hendin discusses the theme of violence in O'Connor's fiction. She states that O'Connor's violent men—such as Tarwater in *The Violent Bear It Away* and The Misfit in "A Good Man Is Hard to Find"—commit acts of violence as a way to express their feelings of impotency, isolation, and rage. Hendin argues that O'Connor's fictional universe depicts life as a perpetual struggle that erupts in violence and subsides in an emotional void.

In O'Connor's heroes, the disease of life has also run its course, rotted all it could, and left only an insensate, durable core of hate. Having emerged from the asylum and prison, Tarwater and the Misfit wreak their vengeance on society.

If violence in the social realist novels in the Thirties reflected the horror of life in Marxist terms, violence in O'Connor's work reflects a more modern brutality. O'Connor's most violent men have been so crushed by life that they suffer with remarkable passivity the alarming pity or open contempt of a society that does not value the "sanctity" of hermaphrodites or psychic freaks. They can never fully shout out their rage at any of the Authorities who shut them up in asylums, jails, or on isolated farms; who demand they analyze themselves, and whose pity or compassion render them still more impotent. It is only in acts of violence that they give voice to their mute fury.

Even in their violence O'Connor's heroes are estranged from their inmost rage. O'Connor always gives their fury a detached, oblique quality. The Misfit, for example, murders

a woman who calls him "one of her babies" and who represents all the forces of Southern tradition and society. Yet he
"does pretty" throughout the mass murder. He speaks po-
litely and murders the grandmother after declaring there
was no finer woman than his mother. Similarly, in O'Connor's brilliant story, "Revelation," Mary Grace tolerates her
mother in a polite silence while she grows more and more
enraged by her mother's double, Mrs. Turpin. Violence toward a stranger lets both misfits express their fury and remain detached from its source at the same time. It both expresses and controls their anger.

Violence springs out of an immense, chaotic inner rage
and imposes a kind of order on it. In a sense O'Connor's heroes murder to create order, justice, and equilibrium. As the
Misfit put it, to "make what all I done wrong" equal to "what
all I gone through in punishment." His murder not only
equalizes his crimes and his punishment, it establishes
many kinds of order. The Misfit's murder proves that he has
resolved his doubts about whether Christ raised the dead.
He confronts his own uncertainty with an absolute, irrevo-
cable act. Similarly Motes kills Layfield, who has a wife, six
children, and tuberculosis and who impersonates Motes in
order to earn three dollars. He parodies Motes's sanctity out
of necessity and not conviction. By killing the false image of
himself, or perhaps an aspect of himself that acts out of
sheer self-interest, Motes remains the only true prophet.
Similarly by drowning Bishop, young Tarwater tries to prove
he is free from both his uncles; by corrupting Norton, Johnson tries to prove to Sheppard that his grandfather was
right—he is evil and damned and not simply misguided. De-
manding neither hope nor salvation, O'Connor's heroes
need only certainty. And all they can know absolutely,
"know for sure," is isolation, rage, and death.

O'Connor's hero comes most alive as he liberates his otherwise passive and silent rage. He tries to murder his way
out of his own abyss, to escape, through moments of self-
transcendence in violence, the pervasive feeling of nothingness. At the moment of his most brutal act, he is able to
break with a past in which he has been despised, scorned,
and ostracized. If he is unable to understand the symbolic
verbal world around him, he is able to answer it in a concrete act of repudiation. He imposes a kind of simplicity on
the confusion about him, certainty on a time of flexible

truths, a floodlight on a kaleidoscope. He hacks a kind of value out of a world where value is all too elusive—a value that, emerging from his own experience, is invariably an affirmation of hate, destruction, and revenge.

Confusion and certainty, alienation and violence appear together in style as well as in theme. O'Connor's style often conflicts with the action she describes and reflects both the emotional flatness of her work and its theme of affectless violence. For example, rigid and stereotyped language often describes the most chaotic, extraordinary events. The Misfit's language abounds in the phrases of politeness: "Yes mam," "I pre-chate that, lady," "Nome," "Would you mind stepping back in them woods there with them?," "I'm sorry I don't have a shirt before you ladies," and "I'll look and see terrectly." His speech is punctuated by the sound of shots from the glen where the family is being murdered.

Like Motes, the Misfit is fond of making absolute statements. As Motes insists that "blasphemy is the way to truth, . . . and there's no other way whether you understand it or not," so the Misfit says there is "no finer" woman than his mother and his father was "pure gold." His absolute statements only diminish when, talking about his doubt of Christ, they change into conditional sentences of an if/then pattern. Although the change in syntax does reflect his confusion, a rigid logical pattern is still maintained. "If He did what He said, then . . . throw away everything and follow Him . . . if He didn't, then . . . enjoy the few minutes you got left . . . If I had of been there, I would of known. . . ." The shots he fires, in effect, resolve the conditional sentences and end his doubts. His next words are an imperative, "Take her off and throw her where you thrown the others."

Images of burial or entrapment define every kind of human relation in O'Connor's incredibly hostile universe. It is not only social institutions, social workers, other people in general, and controlling parents in particular who can trap you; the very fact of growing up can do it. Images of entrapment often define adult life to a child. For example, as a boy, Hazel Motes talks his way into a tent for adults only at a country fair. Looking for his father, he finds instead a nude blonde woman lying in a velvet box. The tent seems an image for the adult world and the blonde in her coffin one for what he will find there: sex and death or, perhaps, death-inducing sex. In "A Temple of the Holy Ghost," the unnamed child heroine remembers an "adults only" tent decorated with stiff, painted figures who remind her of Christian martyrs. She daydreams about them trapped by Romans and waiting to have their tongues cut out. (A distinctively O'Connor association of martyrdom with silence.) Her image of Christians and Romans suggests the most prevalent relationship between people of all ages in O'Connor's fiction: oppressors and oppressed, murderers and victims.

The body is the worst of O'Connor's oppressors. It is a trap more profound than an unknown adult future or the power of Romans over Christians. Many of O'Connor's heroes are turned into psychic cripples by their bodies, or are literally buried alive in their own defective flesh. Never transcended or transformed by the spirit, the body often defines the self and expresses the form of the mind. In "Good Country People," Joy is not only forced to live with her mother in isolation because of her weak heart and artificial leg, she also seems compelled to define herself by them. Naming herself Hulga because it suits her body better than Joy, she names herself after her deformity, letting her artificial leg shape her identity. When the infamous Bible salesman steals it, he steals her essence, leaving her selfless among the red clay hills that loom around her like prison walls. Her deformity not only dictates her image of herself but also shapes her mother's view:

> She thought of her still as a child because it tore her heart to think instead of the poor stout girl in her thirties who had never danced a step or had any *normal* good times

Images of entrapment by the body frequently occur in connection with mechanical aids such as Hulga's artificial leg, Johnson's orthopedic shoe, Rayber's hearing aid, and dental braces worn by those innumerable ugly adolescent girls who populate O'Connor's South. Sorry and defective, the body must rely on steel and plastic to make it beautiful or even functional.

These devices are supposed to lessen and eliminate deformity, the overwhelming reality of O'Connor's heroes. Yet they either increase it or do nothing to diminish it. Hulga's leg in no way lessens her deformity, Rayber's hearing aid hears nothing essentially true. In the most significant moment of his life, the moment when he knows Bishop may scream if Tarwater tries to kill him, "he lay with his eyes closed as if listening to something he could hear only when his hearing aid was off. He sensed that he waited for a cataclysm." Similarly, Johnson refuses the orthopedic shoe that will reduce his limp and prefers to walk in pain, treating his foot "as if it were a sacred object." And none of those dental braces ever comes off.

In images of isolation and entrapment, O'Connor defines a world where life is a perpetual struggle, erupting in acts of violence, subsiding in an emotional void. In her earlier work, her themes evolve as a conflict between the present and the past variously expressed in social, religious, and psychological terms. Opposing images of rural and urban life express the social conflict while the religious one appears as a contrast between a sense of absolutes and damnation, and a secular, relativistic belief in human perfectibility. On a more philosophic plane, O'Connor offers an account of the mind/body problem in Milledgevillese and, psychologically, she describes the conflict between the past and present as a struggle between parent and child. Haze's double glance is frozen into a theme recurring throughout her work: the immobilization of a character before a present that is unfathomable—the leap through the window of a moving train, or a sense of his past felt in terms of disease, decay, suffering, and entrapment. While her sheer consistency of thought may seem irritating and mechanical, it cannot be attributed to banality of style or feeling.

O'Connor wrote about what she knew best: what it means to be a living contradiction. For her it meant an eternal cheeriness and loathing for life; graciousness and fear of human contact; acquiescence and enduring fury. Whether through some great effort of the will, or through some more mysterious and unconscious force, she created from that strife a powerful art, an art that was both a release and a vindication for her life. From the conflict she lived she created an uneasy alliance of the traditional and the modern where familiar Southern or Christian preoccupations explode in unexpected and unconventional directions.

If she set out to make morals, to praise the old values, she ended by engulfing all of them in an icy violence. If she began by mocking or damning her murderous heroes, she ended by exalting them. She grew to celebrate the liberating power of destruction. O'Connor became more and more the pure poet of the Misfit, the oppressed, the psychic cripple, the freak—of all of those who are martyred by silent fury and redeemed through violence.

O'Connor's Use of the Grotesque

Carter W. Martin

Like other writers who were part of the Southern Gothic literary tradition, Flannery O'Connor accentuated the grotesque in her work. In the following article, excerpted from his book *The True Country: Themes in the Fiction of Flannery O'Connor*, Carter W. Martin asserts that O'Connor uses the grotesque to signify the moral and spiritual failings of her characters. Furthermore, he writes, O'Connor employs grotesque imagery to demonstrate how humanity's physical presence has desecrated nature. Martin contends that O'Connor's representations of the grotesque reveal her preoccupation with the ugliness of reality.

Grotesqueness is so pervasive in [Flannery O'Connor's] stories and novels that it may be considered as part of the texture of her fiction.

. . . Grotesqueness is often used to indicate the moral and spiritual conditions of the characters. Several classifications of such images may be found: (1) deformity and feeblemindedness, (2) illness and disease, (3) animal imagery, and (4) machine imagery. Deformed characters are relatively few, and their general meaning fairly consistent: their conditions reflect spiritual incompleteness or lameness. Mr. Shiftlet in "The Life You Save May Be Your Own" has only one arm, Hulga Hopewell in "Good Country People" wears an artificial leg, and Rufus Johnson in "The Lame Shall Enter First" has a clubfoot; each is in some way a moral derelict. An excellent example of this meaning of deformity is given in an image of dismemberment in *The Violent Bear It Away;* Mason Tarwater is telling his great-nephew that the boy's mother was a whore:

Excerpted from *The True Country: Themes in the Fiction of Flannery O'Connor*, by Carter W. Martin. Copyright © 1968 by Carter W. Martin. Reprinted with permission from Vanderbilt University Press.

He knew what they were and to what they were liable to come, and just as Jezebel was discovered by dogs, an arm here and a foot there, so said his great-uncle, it had almost been with his own mother and grandmother. The two of them, along with his grandfather, had been killed in an automobile crash, leaving only the schoolteacher alive in that family.

On the other hand, deformity may exist to demonstrate that man's condition is normally corrupt and that he is better off in accepting it, as the hermaphrodite does in "A Temple of the Holy Ghost," and as the one-armed good Samaritan implicitly does in *Wise Blood* when he helps Hazel Motes to start his broken-down car and refuses any payment from Hazel, who is apparently physically sound. Feeblemindedness is most often associated with innocence, as Bishop in *The Violent Bear It Away* and Lucynell Crater in "The Life You Save May Be Your Own" indicate.

The imagery of illness and disease is never ambiguous, but it might convey different and opposite meanings from one story to another. That cancer on Mr. Paradise's ear in "The River" cannot be healed signifies his internal lack of health; this is reiterated in his mockery of the healing at the river and of religion in general. Mrs. Connin's husband, in the same story, suffers from stomach ulcers and, in spite of her advice, will not thank Jesus or anyone else for the portion of his stomach remaining after surgery. In "A Circle in the Fire" the ignorant and narrow Mrs. Pritchard is thankful that she has nothing more wrong with her than four abscessed teeth, but the reader is aware of a deeper abscess. Even extreme age is a form of illness of the body as well as the soul in "A Late Encounter with the Enemy"; General Sash's most startling line and his most convincing indication of life is his vilification of everything: "God damn every goddam thing to hell." In "A Stroke of Good Fortune," Ruby Hill considers pregnancy not as a sacred responsibility to bring forth new life, but as an illness to which even heart trouble would be preferable; at other times she deludes herself that her pains are from gas. Conversely, the grotesque stories told by Mrs. Pritchard in "A Circle in the Fire" about a woman who gave birth while in an iron lung are startling images illustrating the remarkable endurance of one woman determined to fulfill her feminine role in spite of the most formidable obstacle. A similar juxtaposition within the narrative of "Good Country People" gives meaning to Mrs.

Freeman's revolting chatter about her daughter Carramae's morning sickness in terms of Hulga Hopewell's sterility and her cynical intention to use sex as a weapon by seducing the representative of good country people, the Bible salesman. Asbury Fox's undulant fever in "The Enduring Chill" and Mrs. McIntyre's nervous disorder in "The Displaced Person" signify their poor spiritual health. Mrs. Greenleaf claims to have used prayer healing to rid one man of worms when "half his gut was eat out," and Tarwater believes that the nagging of his religious dedication is worms. The self-inflicted blindness of Hazel Motes is the sign of his submission to God.

O'CONNOR DISCUSSES THE GROTESQUE

O'Connor believed that the term "grotesque" was often used pejoratively to describe writers who were fascinated with the ugly, freakish, or deformed. However, as she explains in this excerpt from a speech given to Wesleyan College for Women in 1960, the grotesque serves an important purpose in fiction.

When we look at a good deal of serious modern fiction, and particularly Southern fiction, we find this quality about it that is generally described, in a pejorative sense, as grotesque. Of course, I have found that anything that comes out of the South is going to be called grotesque by the Northern reader, unless it is grotesque, in which case it is going to be called realistic. But . . . we may leave such misapplications aside and consider the kind of fiction that may be called grotesque with good reason, because of a directed intention that way on the part of the author.

In these grotesque works, we find that the writer has made alive some experience which we are not accustomed to observe every day, or which the ordinary man may never experience in his ordinary life. We find that connections which we would expect in the customary kind of realism have been ignored, that there are strange skips and gaps which anyone trying to describe manners and customs would certainly not have left. Yet the characters have an inner coherence, if not always a coherence to their social framework. Their fictional qualities lean away from typical social patterns, toward mystery and the unexpected.

Flannery O'Connor, *Mystery and Manners.* (eds. Sally and Robert Fitzgerald) New York: Farrar, Straus & Giroux, 1969.

Animal imagery describing people traditionally carries pejorative meaning. This is the usual effect of the many comparisons between characters and animals in Flannery O'Connor's work, although in some instances the reader is expected simply to see detail more clearly. The Biblical uncleanliness of swine is perhaps the key to the frequent use of comparisons involving them. Mr. Paradise and the mischievous Connin children are compared to pigs, and Mary Grace calls Mrs. Turpin a wart hog; in *The Violent Bear It Away*, Tarwater says that Bishop will rot like a hog. Although the complexity of these images varies from story to story, all of them point to the essentially fallen and corrupt, sometimes the unrelievedly unclean, nature of man. The same point pervades the many descriptions of Enoch Emery in *Wise Blood;* at one point he is seen crouching in the shrubbery like an animal on all fours and in another instance he walks "down the street as if he were led by a silent melody or by one of those whistles that only dogs hear." Enoch envies the animals at the zoo; he sometimes imagines what it would feel like to be one of them and achieves his own grotesque triumph when he imbrutes himself in the gorilla outfit of Gonga. Other examples of animal imagery arise, not from the corrupt nature of the characters so described, but from the corruption of the vision of the one who apprehends them in grotesque fashion. Mark Fortune sees his daughter's entire family as a chorus of frogs around the dinner table. Ruby Hill is revolted by Mr. Jerger, the old man who lives in the apartment building; to her, he looks like a goat, and his odor is "like putting her nose under a buzzard's wing." Actually, neither Mr. Jerger nor the Pittses are so animal-like as the ones who describe them.

Characters associated with machines usually have severely limited human responses and function mechanically rather than humanly. In *Wise Blood*, this deficiency is made broadly applicable to society in general through the juxtaposition of a man who hawks potato peelers and Asa Hawks, who merchandises Christian salvation. Hazel Motes tries to believe that his automobile is sufficient to save him, and the degenerate Sabbath Lily Hawks turns her head "as if it worked on a screw." Enoch Emery's heart is said to beat with a sound like a motorcycle racing around an enclosed sphere at the county fair, and in *The Violent Bear It Away* Rayber's heart is often compared to a machine. . . .

HUMAN DESECRATION OF NATURE

If man's jaded point of view distorts nature, so does his physical presence desecrate the landscape, as the littered plot of land where Tilman does business in "A View of the Woods" reveals. In *The Violent Bear It Away*, T. Fawcett Meeks and Tarwater stop at a filling station on the outskirts of the city, "a gaping concrete mouth with two red gas pumps set in front of it and a small glass office toward the back"; its grotesqueness is repeated in descriptions of the city throughout the stories and novels. In *Wise Blood* Hazel Motes looks upon a landscape scarred by the evidence of man's presence.

> The highway was ragged with filling stations and trailer camps and roadhouses. After a while there were stretches where red gulleys dropped off on either side of the road and behind them there were patches of field buttoned together with 666 posts. The sky leaked over all of it and then it began to leak into the car. The head of a string of pigs appeared snout-up over the ditch and he had to screech to a stop and watch the rear of the last pig disappear shaking into the ditch on the other side. He started the car again and went on. He had the feeling that everything he saw was a broken-off piece of some giant blank thing that he had forgotten had happened to him. A black pick-up truck turned off a side road in front of him. On the back of it an iron bed and a chair and table were tied, and on top of them, a crate of barred-rock chickens.

The desecrated landscape is one manifestation of Flannery O'Connor's preoccupation with the ugliness of reality. She speaks of this kind of grotesqueness in a letter to Sister Mary Alice: "If you have a detail that is just the traditional kind of prettiness, reject it, and look for one that is closer to the heart of the matter, that is a little more grotesque, but that gives us a better idea of the reality of the thing." To the writer with a close, hard, objective vision, the world contains a great deal of unpleasant reality that need not be distorted to appear grotesque. When man is seen against the background of Christian idealism, his characteristics, actions, and features of his personally created environment reveal, sometimes revoltingly, his fallen state. In "A Circle in the Fire" for instance, the common insolence and vulgarity of one of the boys conveys such an effect:

> The large boy was stretched out in the hammock with his wrists crossed under his head and the cigarette stub in the center of his mouth. He spit it out in an arc just as Mrs. Cope

came around the corner of the house with a plate of crackers. She stopped instantly as if a snake had been slung in her path.

In "The Life You Save May Be Your Own," Mr. Shiftlet offers Mrs. Crater a piece of chewing gum: "she only raised her upper lip to indicate she had no teeth." Neither of these actions is distorted; they are a part of the ordinary ugliness and vulgarity that attend life in this world. There is an equal absence of distortion in the picture of Sulk, whose tongue hangs out and describes small circles as he examines a photograph of Mr. Guizac's young cousin. Similar examples may be found throughout the stories and novels.

Even when grotesqueness is rendered with the help of comparisons, there is such aptness that one feels the grotesqueness is the result of actuality, not the vehicle of the metaphor. In *Wise Blood,* for example, there are three women who are "dressed like parrots," and a dining car steward who moves about "like a crow." Mrs. Flood has "race-horse legs" and "hair clustered like grapes on her brow."

In *The Violent Bear It Away* Rayber searches for a gift to placate Tarwater after discarding the boy's disreputable clothes:

> He stopped for gas at a pink stucco filling station where pottery and whirligigs were sold. While the car was being filled, he got out and looked for something to take as a peace offering, for he wanted the encounter to be pleasant if possible. His eye roved over a shelf of false hands, imitation buck teeth, boxes of simulated dog dung to put on the rug, wooden plaques with cynical mottos burnt on them. Finally he saw a combination corkscrew-bottleopener that fit in the palm of the hand. He bought it and left.

This is the ludicrous world as Flannery O'Connor sees it; her selection of detail is not the caricaturist's method of distortion, but she sees the actual horror and ugliness of the world. Its grotesqueness results from her technique of drawing large, of seeing reality as if examining nearby phenomena through a telescope or as if directing her readers' eyes through a microscope to show them what should be visible to the naked eye. Whether grotesqueness in her work is a part of the Gothic impulse, whether it is in the distorted vision of spiritually myopic characters, whether it is in the spectacle of grotesque behavior brought about by the characters' lack of knowledge of themselves and their true country, or whether grotesqueness is simply the everyday ugliness that exists as a testament to the disparity between this world and that of the ideal, Flannery O'Connor's purpose is always the same: to see actuality without undue sentimental or romantic regret that paradise is not of this world, and to demonstrate that for all its horror, life here is merely passage by the dragon as one goes to the Father of Souls. This passage, she believes, is the concern of any story of depth and demands courage on the part of the reader. The storyteller too must have considerable courage to present the horror of the passage as he sees it.

O'Connor Questions the Value of Beauty

Edward Kessler

The following selection, excerpted from Edward Kessler's book *Flannery O'Connor and the Language of Apocalypse,* examines the absence of beauty in O'Connor's fiction. By writing about physically unappealing characters instead of beautiful ones, claims Kessler, O'Connor attempts to direct her readers' attention away from the superficiality of appearances. In O'Connor's world, appearing ugly has no correlation with ugliness of character.

The absence of superficial beauty in O'Connor's work discomforts many of her readers who are, perhaps, looking for beautiful products rather than the beauty of process. Her notoriously unattractive characters resemble caterpillars evolving into butterflies, and as she forces our attention to a lower stage of the evolutionary process she makes us acknowledge that beauty inhabits *all* acts of becoming. By seeking out only the butterfly and ignoring the caterpillar, we run the risk of reducing the beautiful to the picturesque, in the same way that clichés mask genuine feelings. Beauty like goodness cannot be *identified* with an object—a person or objects in the natural world; it is a way of seeing an object. The grandmother in "A Good Man is Hard to Find" seems blind to both art and nature. She calls attention to a scene, but she cannot see it: "Oh, look at the cute little pickaninny! . . . Wouldn't that make a picture, now? . . . If I could paint, I'd paint that picture." To the unseeing eye, even poverty is picturesque.

Early in *Wise Blood,* the unattractive Sabbath Lily tells a story about a woman with good looks who tried to get rid of her ugly child. But the child kept returning, until the woman and her lover "strangled it with a silk stocking and hung it up in the chimney."

"It didn't give her any peace after that, though. Everything she looked at was that child. Jesus made it beautiful to haunt her. She couldn't lie with that man without she saw it, staring through the chimney at her, shining through the brick in the middle of the night."

"My Jesus," Haze muttered.

"She didn't have nothing but good looks," she said in the loud fast voice. "That ain't enough. No sirree."

More than one reader has been offended by O'Connor's refusal to create pleasant images, comforting similes like Eudora Welty's. One reader finds her view of life "repugnant," not only because she writes about unappealing people but because she compels her readers to embrace them in spite of—or rather, because of—their ugliness. Like goodness, beauty can be released from its physical confinement by metaphor; and, by directing our attention to a lower stage of an evolutionary process, O'Connor ensures that, undistracted by appearances, we will begin to recognize a power that supersedes all aesthetic categories. Good looks are truly not enough; it is the mysterious power "shining through the brick in the middle of the night" that rescues us from the confining forms of materialism. If, as Roman Guardini says, "Evil is what is absolutely superfluous," then the beautiful power of goodness is that it is absolutely essential. By her cultivation of the ugly, O'Connor keeps us from *identifying* ourselves with the material. Instead, a piece of passing description can awaken us to the power *within* the natural world: "The trees were full of silver-white sunlight and the meanest of them sparkled." The power, capable of "shining through the brick in the middle of the night," inhabits the trees, making them sparkle. The meanest of O'Connor's characters sparkles as well.

Accepting an essentially flawed human nature, O'Connor questions the value of superficial beauty, as she does the value of all appearances. The "beauty contest" that takes place in "The Partridge Festival" seems as trivial as the town's motto ("Beauty is Our Money Crop") is materialistic. Like a prophet, O'Connor combats the dangerous illusion that good looks—like good works—are enough, and she further refuses to tolerate our contentment with ourselves as we are—and not as we can be. At times, O'Connor resembles Gulliver after his return from Brobdingnag, when he cannot look in a mirror without comparing his inferior physical image with that of the superior giants he remembers. O'Connor shares Gulliver's wonder and laughter at human pride and absurdity, but she also keeps in mind the lesson in perspective Gulliver learned from his travels: "Our beauty is only apparent; our disproportion real.". . .

O'Connor shares with many modern poets a mistrust of the word beautiful. In "Good Country People," Mrs. Hopewell laments that her "bloated, rude and squint-eyed" daughter has changed her "beautiful name" Joy to Hulga, which she finds "the ugliest name in the language." The names themselves contrast the girls perverse need for an individual identity with her mother's desire for social harmony: the agreeable manner, the "pleasant expression." Even the word "joy" in Mrs. Hopewell's vocabulary suggests self-satisfaction more than the overpowering force of bliss or rapture. Mrs. Hopewell would disguise and subordinate the self in order to conform to things-as-they-are, a beauty of surfaces. Looking at her daughter, she thinks: "There was nothing wrong with her face that a pleasant expression wouldn't help." And the author underscores Mrs. Hopewell's basic dishonesty: "Mrs. Hopewell said that people who looked at the bright side of things would be beautiful even if they were not." Mrs. Hopewell's clichés, the common coin of social exchange, confine her to a temporal community and block her way toward the recognition of Mystery. In this relatively early story, O'Connor presents unproductive extremes. Hulga, disillusioned, contemptuous of her surroundings, has "achieved" blindness. By not paying "any close attention to her surroundings," she alienates herself from the power operating within nature and can therefore "see through to nothing." And her mother, who cannot penetrate surfaces, sees nothing beyond.

The same opposing pair—the "stylish lady" and the fat, scowling daughter who has "ugly looks for everybody"—appears in O'Connor's masterful later story, "Revelation," but here the false opposition is mediated by Ruby Turpin, a third character who holds center stage, and who discovers the life-giving power that lies behind all natural and social forms. Although we will look at this story later, in connection with O'Connor's endings, here we can point out that mystery can come to life only when customary ways of seeing beauty and ugliness are disrupted. With a "friendly smile," Ruby Turpin, like Mrs. Hopewell, accepts the demands of a polite society, its hierarchy and conventions, but when she begins to doubt the value of her social identity, she starts a movement that can free the mystery confined by superficial forms, whether natural or linguistic.

> What if Jesus had said, "All right, you can be white-trash or a nigger or ugly!"

> Mrs. Turpin felt an awful pity for the girl, though she thought it was one thing to be ugly and another to act ugly.

Within prescribed limits, Mrs. Turpin will entertain some displacement in the chain of being, but she does not anticipate a change of species: her antagonist Mary Grace causes her to ask not "Am I a hog?" but "How am I a hog?" Even the adage she uses, "One thing to be ugly and another to act ugly," resonates with more than the obvious plea for social adjustment: *acting ugly* in the world's eyes is a metaphor for the violence necessary to alter consciousness and to begin the evolution toward true beauty and goodness, and *appearing* ugly has no verifiable correlation with ugliness of being. Only Satan *is* ugly—and he cannot be described except by images that trivialize his power.

Like Coleridge's Ancient Mariner, who by his violent tale of suffering alienates the Wedding Guest from his comfortable social role, ugly Mary Grace through her violent act teaches Ruby Turpin that beauty is not a stable surface to be appreciated but a hidden power that demands the destruction of social and linguistic preconceptions before it can be seen. Believing that she has achieved immunity from the world's ugliness through her good works and proper behavior, Ruby finds even her clichés disproved. "It never hurt anyone to smile" is belied by the "angry red swelling above her eye"; and Ruby Turpin with the "friendly smile" will be scowling like Mary Grace when she returns home: "Claud slept. She scowled at the ceiling." However, even before she reaches home, Ruby knows that her way of seeing has been radically altered. Her secure definition of beauty has been violated:

> As their pick-up truck turned into their own dirt road and made the crest of the hill, Mrs. Turpin gripped the window ledge and looked out suspiciously. The land sloped *gracefully* down through a field *dotted* with lavender weeds and at the start of the rise their *small* yellow frame house, with its *little flower beds* spread out around it like a *fancy* apron, sat *primly* in its *accustomed* place between two giant hickory trees. She would not have been startled to see a burnt wound between two blackened chimneys [my emphasis].

O'Connor describes both a physical place, and a condition of being, and Ruby Turpin's beautiful has been exposed as the pretty, the picturesque. The imagined "ugly" violence threatens only the feeble, ephemeral shapes she has imposed on the world. Ruby's expanding vision even burns through the false piety of her Negro help who attempt to reinforce the status quo, her earlier sense of beauty as social conformity: "You des as sweet and pretty as you can be" and "Jesus satisfied with her." Both Ruby's satisfaction with appearances and her self-satisfaction have been altered, as a preparation for her apocalyptic vision that arrives at the story's end.

By undermining the value of beautiful and ugly as terms for realizing the mystery of human existence, O'Connor opens the way to apocalypse. In her quest to reach beyond human assessments of human worth, she felt compelled to expose all phantom representations of interior being. The two Roman Catholic priests who very briefly figure in her body of work are far from idealized: one has a "homely red face" and is absent-minded, if not senile; the other is blind in one eye, deaf in one ear, and has a "grease spot on his vest." O'Connor wrote to a friend: "Maryat's niece asked her why I made Mary Grace so ugly. Because Flannery loves her, said Maryat. Very perceptive girl." Natural objects are not beautiful without our attention or, in Blake's words, "Where man is absent, nature is barren." By implicating her readers in her own love for ugly misfits, O'Connor introduces us to the process of seeing, and thereby provides a kind of redemption for flawed images. Mother Teresa said of her job of caring for the ugly, diseased, and dying of Calcutta: "It's beautiful work."

CHAPTER 3

A Critical Selection

READINGS ON
FLANNERY O'CONNOR

Psychology in "Everything That Rises Must Converge"

Preston M. Browning Jr.

Preston M. Browning Jr., professor of English at the University of Illinois at Chicago Circle at the time this article was written, is the author of two books: *Adversity and Grace: Studies in Recent American Literature* and *Flannery O'Connor*, from which the following selection is excerpted. In this selection, Browning argues that the story "Everything That Rises Must Converge" exemplifies O'Connor's keen understanding of human psychology. Julian, the story's protagonist, scorns his mother because she represents to him the racist and narrow-minded culture of the South. However, writes Browning, Julian's hostility toward his mother is simply a mechanism by which he avoids acknowledging his own biases and inadequacies. Only when his mother dies and Julian recognizes his dependence on her can he begin to develop the capacity for self-love and love for others.

In Flannery O'Connor's posthumous volume of stories, *Everything That Rises Must Converge* (1965), subject and setting are very much a part of the contemporary South. Economic growth is under way, and its partisans are feverishly engaged as midwives to "progress" ("A View of the Woods"); racial integration is a fact increasingly difficult to ignore, and white Southerners of all classes are forced to assume some attitude toward it ("Everything That Rises Must Converge"). The upheavals wrought by World War II and the Korean conflict have unsettled class lines, and the sons of tenant farmers are on their way to becoming "society"

("Greenleaf"); the dispersion of poor whites throughout the urban North is well advanced, constituting opportunity for many of the young but exile in an alien and hostile land for the elderly ("Judgement Day"). And, as in the novel, *The Violent Bear It Away,* the techniques of modern psychology are being liberally applied by social worker-types reared on progressive philosophies ("The Lame Shall Enter First"). Wherever one turns in these stories, he encounters evidence of Flannery O'Connor's sensitivity to the changes which her region was undergoing during the late 1950s and early 1960s.

As always, Miss O'Connor brought to these subjects an intelligence keenly alive to the complexities of the human mind—its subterfuges, its self-deceptions, its seemingly inexhaustible capacity for rationalization. In her two novels and in such early stories as "Good Country People," "The Life You Save May Be Your Own," and "The Artificial Nigger," she had demonstrated an astonishingly mature grasp of the dynamics of human psychology. Yet something new (in degree if not in kind) seems to distinguish the stories of the second collection: an almost clinical understanding of certain forms of neurosis. The title story, for example, is a virtual case study of what psychoanalysts would describe as denial and projection.

The narrative itself is simple enough: Julian and his mother travel by bus to the Y in order that she may attend a reducing class. Contemptuous of his mother, from whose values and prejudices he thinks he has freed himself, Julian attempts unsuccessfully to befriend a Negro man and indulges in malicious glee when a large Negro woman boards the bus wearing a hat identical to the one his mother has on. As they leave the bus together, Mrs. Chestny offers a penny to the Negro woman's small son and is knocked to the sidewalk by the infuriated Negress. After pointing out to his mother that she has been taught a proper lesson, Julian discovers that she is dying and runs for help in a last futile effort to delay his entrance in the "world of guilt and sorrow."

A SAD YOUNG MAN

Like many of the sad young men of Flannery O'Connor's last stories, the protagonist of "Everything That Rises Must Converge" wants desperately to distinguish himself from everything in the South which he finds morally, intellectually, and aesthetically repugnant: its racism, its nostalgia for the glorious past, its (to him) petty concern with manners, its barren intellectual life, its insufferably banal social intercourse. (Julian is cast from the same mold that produced the rebellious "artistic" or "intellectual" sons of "The Enduring Chill," "The Comforts of Home," and "Greenleaf." Julian, Asbury, Thomas, and Wesley make up a quartet of angry, frustrated individuals caught in "late adolescent impotence so acute that they can direct their hostility only against their protective, and oftentimes patronizing and controlling mothers.)

Julian wants to be different, and since everything about the South which affronts his sense of decency and decorum is symbolized by his mother, Julian wants especially to be different from his mother. Merely being different, however, is not sufficient; his hatred for all that his mother epitomizes is so venomous that he must constantly insult it. As it is impossible to insult the entire Southern ethos, Julian is reduced to the expediency of humiliating and insulting his mother. But Julian's relation to his mother, like his relation to the South itself, is less unambiguous than he would like to imagine. What he thinks he detests, he also loves and longs for. What he believes he is totally free of, he is, in fact, fearfully dependent upon.

While Miss O'Connor undoubtedly portrays the bad faith of Julian as the more damning, it must be conceded that there is something exasperating about his mother. She is one of those legendary Southern matrons of "aristocratic" birth who, though forced to live in relative poverty, continues to insist upon a distinction which she believes birth has conferred upon her. Though she must use the now-integrated public transportation system and must associate at the YWCA with women of a lower social class, she insists that because she "'knows who she is,'" she "'can be gracious to anybody.'" Indeed, it is this assumption that the glue which holds society together is a certain politeness and openness of manner—almost always, however, practiced with a degree of unconscious condescension—which enables Julian's mother to face the unpleasant alterations in her external circumstances with a calm and cheerful assurance that she herself at least has not changed. It is her ardent faith in the primacy of manners, in fact, which is one of the sources of the conflict between Julian and his mother. She insists that authentic culture is "'in the heart . . . and in how you do things and how you do things is because of who you *are*.'" Julian's attitude provides the starkest contrast, since he maintains that with the new fluidity of class structure, his mother's graciousness counts for nothing. "'Knowing who you are is good for one generation only,'" he declares. "'You haven't the foggiest idea where you stand now or who you are.'"

JULIAN'S AMBIVALENCE ABOUT THE SOUTH

Naturally, Julian is convinced that he knows where *he* is. Yet he is in fact far more pitifully confused than his mother. In him Flannery O'Connor has drawn a devastating portrait of the young white "liberal" Southerner who is doing all of the supposedly right things for the wrong reasons. Conceited in his assurance that he is free of his mother's prejudices and her unrealistic attachment to a dead past, Julian betrays in every gesture and word his thoroughly ambivalent attitudes toward the principal objects of her bigotry (Negroes) and her nostalgia (the ancestral home). How small the distance is he has put between himself and the heritage which he condemns is suggested in this description of his feelings about the family mansion he had once seen as a child.

> He never spoke of it without contempt or thought of it without longing. He had seen it once. . . . The double stairways had rotted and been torn down. Negroes were living [in] it. But it remained in his mind as his mother had known it. It appeared in his dreams regularly. . . . He preferred its threadbare elegance to anything he could name.

In some way reminiscent of Quentin Compson's tortured exclamation at the conclusion of *Absalom, Absalom!* [a novel by William Faulkner], "I don't hate it, I don't hate it" (the "it" referring to the South), Julian's reveries reflect much of the ambivalence but little of the profundity of Quentin's attitude toward the traditional South. For, whereas Quentin stands much closer to the great decisive events which have shaped Southern history and must grapple existentially with their meaning, as well as with the meaning of his own family's former glory and present decadence, Julian is a child of the 1950s and sixties, and, as such, faces the quite different problem of establishing personal identity in a South for which neither the grandeur nor the guilt of the past are ever-present, haunting realities. Yet the tradition which his mother represents, while attenuated and diluted, is nonetheless a factor with which he must reckon. Wishing to assert his independence from his mother, he vehemently proclaims his independence of the cultural heritage from which she derives *her* identity. But as he finds his present life and surroundings drab and humiliating, he is forced against his conscious will to identify with that very way of life which he can neither appropriate completely, as his mother thinks she has done, nor repudiate completely, as he would like to believe he has done.

The confusion of his attitude toward the Southern past is recapitulated and underscored in his ambivalent feelings toward his mother, whom he considers a child, "innocent and untouched by experience," for whose protection he must sacrifice himself. Remote as Julian's mother's world may be from reality, Julian's own fantasy world is even more remote. With his arrogant sense of superiority ("he realized he was too intelligent to be a success"), Julian's habitual way of dealing with the unpleasant aspects of life is to retreat "into the inner compartment of his mind . . . a kind of mental bubble" from which he may judge the intellectual bankruptcy of the rest of mankind. Somewhat like Hulga and very much like Asbury of "The Enduring Chill," Wesley of "Greenleaf," and Thomas of "The Comforts of Home," Julian suffers from a form of neurosis in which his idealized image is threatened by self-doubt and self-pity and can be protected only by maintaining an uncommitted and superior attitude toward the world. At the same time subjecting the world to withering scorn for its failures and fearing to engage the world in creative struggle, Julian withdraws into his bubble where the self is free to judge without making itself vulnerable to judgment.

The viability of Julian's defensive psychological mechanism largely depends upon the availability of someone whom he can continuously belittle and scorn and whose stupidity and phoniness (as judged by him) can serve to point up, by contrast, his own supposedly enlightened and authentic existence. And that person is his mother. But while Julian thus needs his mother, she also poses a constant threat, to the extent that she is able to withstand his attacks and, through simply being what she is, to insinuate the possibility of some radical discrepancy between his idealized image and the actuality of his life. Ultimately, therefore, he must attempt to destroy her or destroy *for* her that system of values which makes her life possible.

On the bus an opportunity of attack presents itself when a white woman moves from a seat next to one just occupied by a Negro man. Ostensibly to "convey his sympathy" but actually to embarrass his mother, Julian crosses the aisle to the vacated seat. Now so situated that he can stare at her as though he were a stranger, Julian experiences a release of tension such as might accompany a declaration of war. Julian now fantasizes about various ways of hurting his mother, though always the conscious intention is "to teach her a lesson." Interestingly, all of his schemes involve Negroes or causes related to Negroes.

Julian's "Liberalism"

Here brief reflection upon Julian's "liberalism" should help to illumine the moral and psychological ramifications of the story. It is clear that Julian uses his putative tolerance and freedom from racial bias as a weapon in the struggle with his mother. What is far worse, he *uses Negroes* for the same purpose. Significantly, Julian has "never been successful in making Negro friends"; the reason for his failure is not difficult to locate, since he all too obviously wishes only to accumulate "some of the better types, . . . ones that looked like professors or ministers or lawyers" to bolster his always tenuous bold upon his self-image as a liberated representative of the "new South." Julian's own latent prejudice begins to show itself when a huge, fierce-looking Negro woman, who could not possibly be mistaken for a member of the Negro intelligentsia, boards the bus and settles in a seat next to his. Julian is "annoyed." Quickly his annoyance turns to elation as he sees the symbolic appropriateness of the two women having "swapped sons" when the woman's small child sits next to his mother. Julian's triumph is completed when he notices that the Negro woman's hat is an exact match of the one his mother is wearing for the first time.

Reveling briefly in his mother's distress, Julian discovers their true relationship after she has been struck to the ground by the hostile Negro woman. Attempting to reinforce the "lesson" with what sounds like a rehearsed lecture, Julian assures his mother that the fury she has just witnessed is not that of a single "uppity Negro woman" but rather that of "the whole colored race which will no longer take your condescending pennies." His speech is lost on his mother, who, calling for "Grampa" and Caroline (the Negro mammy who had cared for her as a child), willingly submits to "a tide of darkness" which carries her swiftly back to the ordered world of childhood and thence to death. Julian, who had moments before wished to prove to his mother she could not expect to be forever dependent upon him, is compelled at last to recognize how total has been his dependence upon her. Crying "Mamma, Mamma!" he throws himself beside her, but "Mamma," whose gaze had earlier scanned his face but recognized nothing there, lies motionless. Last seen racing toward lights which appear to recede beyond his grasp, Julian postpones momentarily "his entry into the world of guilt and sorrow." On this unmistakable Hawthornesque [relating to American writer Nathaniel Hawthorne] note the chronicle of another American Adam is concluded.

THE EXISTENTIAL DILEMMAS OF THE SELF

For a number of reasons the choice of this story to open the collection was a happy one. . . . Like most of the stories in this volume, "Everything That Rises Must Converge" focuses upon the existential dilemmas of the self—its anxiety before the truth of its condition, the contemptible dodges it employs to deceive itself, and the inescapable surge of guilt as the shock of awareness is delivered. But in this tale the social context is broadened, thereby providing a connecting thread to the last story in *A Good Man Is Hard to Find*, "The Displaced Person," in which race relations play a significant role, as well as pointing forward to the other pieces in the present volume, in most of which there is a heightened consciousness of the social ambience within which the awakened individual must live in the presence of grace. Both the title and the story's action give evidence of Flannery O'Connor's growing interest in the movement of the isolated self toward union with others; and while many commentators have maintained that Miss O'Connor uses the line borrowed from [French paleontologist, Jesuit priest, and philosopher] Teilhard de Chardin ironically, I find myself in agreement with those critics who contend that in the narrative of Julian and his mother there is a true convergence, although not a simple one. As the title suggests, the story concerns both rising and converging. Before their bus ride, Julian's mother had spoken of the propriety of Negroes rising, "but on their side of the fence." Her encounter with the outraged woman attests to the rising which has already occurred, as well as the fragility of the fence and the difficulty of maintaining it. But a convergence, albeit a violent one, does take place, and there are numerous hints besides the obvious one of the identical hats, that Julian's mother and the Negro woman are more alike than either would care to admit. If nothing else, the story's action foreshadows a convergence such as that envisaged by Teilhard, who speaks of "courage and resourcefulness" as necessary ingredients in the struggle to overcome "the forces of isolationism, even of repulsion, which seem to drive [men] apart rather than draw them together." Though the results of this particular convergence are quite the opposite of those anticipated by Teilhard when mankind achieves its unity in Christ, and though it would seem that here there is only reinforced isolation and repulsion, emphasis should perhaps be placed upon the pain and cost of both rising and converging. Such emphasis is certainly congruent with Miss O'Connor's belief that redemption is never easy and always involves suffering. The frustration and anger of the Negro woman *and* her courage imply a depth of spirit out of which might someday come the "resourcefulness" requisite for genuine convergence.

But since it is Julian, not the Negro mother, who is the main character, it is his rising and convergence which is central. As in other renditions of the fortunate fall, Julian's calamity will eventually lead, so all the evidence indicates, to "growth of consciousness," to raised sight, to a risen spirit. According to Teilhard de Chardin, growth toward unity with others is the spiritual direction of evolution and is a process to which those with "expanded consciousness" contribute. It is, moreover, the true end of man. "To be fully ourselves it is in . . . the direction of convergence with all the rest, that we must advance—towards the 'other.'" Teilhard distinguishes between individuality and personhood and asserts that the latter can be achieved only by "uniting together. . . . The true ego grows in inverse proportion to 'egoism.'" Insofar as Julian is able to replace his defensive idealized image with a realistic view of the self which obviates the necessity of belittling others in order to enhance the value of the self, to this extent will it be possible for him to attain personhood, a "true ego" capable of proper self-love and proper love of others. The capacity to develop such an ego is the psychological equivalent of the Christian's faith in man's ability to be radically altered by grace, and in the volume as a whole this capacity emerges as a central concern.

The Comic Redemption in "Revelation"

Ralph C. Wood

In the following article, professor Ralph C. Wood examines the change that Ruby Turpin, a cheerful but prejudiced farm wife, undergoes in O'Connor's story "Revelation." Wood contends that when Mary Grace, a contemptuous Wellesley student, attacks and insults Ruby in a doctor's waiting room, Ruby's complacency is shattered and she begins to experience a revelation that is both comic and profound. Wood, a professor of theology and literature at Baylor University in Waco, Texas, is the author of a number of books about religion in literature, including *The Comedy of Redemption: Christian Faith and Comic Vision in Four American Novelists*, from which this article was taken. He is also the editor-at-large for *Christian Century* magazine.

"Revelation" is O'Connor's quintessentially comic story. It concerns a farm woman named Ruby Turpin who has brought her husband Claud to the doctor's office to be treated for a leg ailment. Mrs. Turpin presides over the waiting room with a self-certainty that is wonderfully funny. Unlike the self pitying Mrs. May, Ruby is outgoing and ingratiating. Her disposition is as sparkling and ruddy as her name. Her few facial wrinkles come, in fact, "from laughing too much." Mrs. Turpin can indeed joke about everything, including her own fatness. Her prejudices are, at least initially, far more humorous than monstrous. Even her classification of the other patients according to the shoes they wear is more laughable than contemptible. Her pretensions to gentility cannot be taken seriously, if only because they are so marvellously undermined by her blundering grammar. "Above she and Claud" and "below she and Claud" are the constructions of a mind striving vainly for correctness.

Surely the funniest of Mrs. Turpin's complacencies is her method for dozing off at night. She tries to imagine what kind of woman she might have been had God not made her the splendid person that she is. Ruby envisions Jesus as offering her the bitter choice of being enfleshed as either a "nigger" or "white-trash." Though she would have protested against such equally unpalatable alternatives, Mrs. Turpin confesses that she would finally have chosen to be a dignified black rather than a shameless white: "'All right,' [she would have said to Jesus], 'make me a nigger then—but that don't mean a trashy one.' And he would have made her a neat clean respectable Negro woman, herself but black."

Ruby Turpin is not an ogre of evil. Unlike the self-seeking Grandmother in "A Good Man Is Hard to Find," she does not need someone to shoot her every minute of her life in order to become a good woman. She is much more akin to Julian's mother in "Everything That Rises Must Converge"—a woman who naively accepts the prejudices of her own time and place, who means well rather thin ill, and who views the world according to her own best lights. The problem is, of course, that Mrs. Turpin's best lights—like those of fallen humanity in general—are far from adequate. They do not enable her to see herself as God sees her, and thus as she really is. Ruby needs to learn, therefore, not only the horror of her sin but also—and far more importantly—the wonder of her salvation.

RUBY'S HIERARCHIES OF RACE AND CLASS

Mrs. Turpin's amusing self-satisfaction turns out not to be so innocent as it first may seem. O'Connor uncovers the real terror of evil by showing how it begins guilelessly enough but how, by a strange mutation, it is transformed into something heinously destructive. In her nighttime imaginings, for example, Ruby constructs hierarchies of race and class that are based upon blood and money and property. But then she remembers that there are genteel whites who have lost their possessions, and that there are black doctors who own expensive homes and cars and cattle. The world's refusal to conform to Mrs. Turpin's idea of it poisons her imagination. "Usually by the time she had fallen asleep all the classes of people were moiling and roiling around in her head, and she would dream they were all crammed in together in a box car, being ridden off to be put in a gas oven." This is the working of an incipiently totalitarian mind. As in "The Displaced Person," O'Connor proves that the death camps could have been erected in rural Georgia as surely as in Germany and Poland. Like Mrs. Shortley of the earlier story, Ruby wants the world to be ordered according to her own norms. And if she cannot have her way, she wills to have everything dissolved into the chaos of nihilistic destruction.

Although "Revelation" is a story with a comic beginning and end, it turns very dark and menacing in the middle. What begins as one woman's innocent prejudice and ingenuous self-contentment ends in an arrogance so overweening that it stinks in God's nostrils and thus courts its painful undoing. No longer content inwardly to classify people according to class and dress, Ruby Turpin begins to fling outward insults at the other patients, comparing the cleanliness of her swine to the dirty children in the waiting room. She also reveals how little love there is in her supposed preference for self-respecting blacks over no-count whites: "I sure am tired of buttering up niggers, but you got to love em if you want em to work for you."

Mrs. Turpin's religious sense of service is also revealed to be massively complacent: "To help anybody out that needed it was her philosophy of life. She never spared herself when she found somebody in need, whether they were white or black, trash or decent. And of all that she had to be thankful for, she was most thankful that this was so." Ruby concludes her Pharisaic litany of self-congratulation by praising Christ himself for having created and maintained everything as it is: "Her heart rose. He had not made her a nigger or white-trash or ugly! He had made her herself and given her a little of everything. Jesus, thank you, she said. Thank you thank you thank you!"

AN UNINVITING HANDMAIDEN OF THE LORD

Ruby Turpin meets her nemesis in the form of a Wellesley student who, home from college, is also waiting for the doctor. Her name, not unlike Mary Flannery O'Connor, is Mary Grace. She proves to be a most uninviting handmaiden of the Lord: eaten up with acne, wearing Girl Scout shoes, and brimming with contempt for everything, especially for the falsely grateful Mrs. Turpin. Mary Grace is another of those curdled intellectuals who populate O'Connor's fiction, waiting to spew their soured milk on anything that strikes them as saccharine. She rises to angry action when Ruby crows her final chorus of thankfulness to Jesus for making her life so good. Striking Mrs. Turpin over the eye with a huge psychology text, this demon of wrath flings her roughly to the floor and screams at her: "Go back to hell where you came from, you old warthog."

This is indeed a skewering judgment. The horns of condemnation impale Mrs. May no less severely in "Greenleaf," nor do the eyes of accusation rake Julian any more fiercely in "Everything That Rises Must Converge." And yet the effect of this literal blow to Ruby's head is—for once in O'Connor's fiction—more amusing than horrifying. Mrs. Turpin has indeed received her due, but it is delivered so comically that there is no fear it will have an obliterating effect. Nor is the reader tempted to believe that Mary Grace, as an avenging demon of secular righteousness, stands in better spiritual stead than Ruby. The title of her psychology text (*Human Development*) suggests that she would probably make a reductionist reading of Ruby as a woman "arrested" at one of the early "stages" along the evolutionary path to "maturity." Having no transcendent source for her wrath, Mary Grace has no transcendent hope for her own recovery. We see her for the last time when, having been injected with a tranquilizer, she is taken away to a mental hospital. The ungracious Mary Grace will meet, no doubt, the fate prophesied so crudely by the white-trash woman: "That ther girl is going to be a lunatic, ain't she?"

Ruby Turpin, by contrast, has supernal hope if only because she knows that she has met with supernal judgment. She does not view the attack as the mere insult of a rude and mean-spirited student. Not for a moment does Ruby doubt that this ugly girl is the avenging angel of God. So overwhelming is Ruby's guilt that she expects God's rage to have been visited even upon her farm house: "She would not have been startled to see a burnt wound between two blackened chimneys." Yet Mrs. Turpin's contrition is only momentary. Her tears of meek denial that she is a warthog sent from hell are soon dried into the white-hot fury of metaphysical rebellion. Whether to her husband, to the black farm workers, or to the circumambient air itself, Ruby makes an embittered protest against the God who has ceased to uphold the established order, and who has unleashed his judgment upon her and all the things she stands for: "Occasionally she raised her fist and made a small stabbing motion over her chest as if she was defending her innocence to invisible guests who were like the comforters of Job, reasonable-seeming but wrong."

Mrs. Turpin is unable, alas, to convince anyone of her innocence, and herself least of all. Claud's kisses mean nothing. The false flattery of the Negro tenants is more maddening still. When Ruby tells the black laborers about the indignity she has suffered in the waiting room, they enrage her with their feigned compliments. Like the black laborers in "The Enduring Chill," these Negroes are adept at the art of "signifying"—of saying polite words that are loaded with venom. Not only is she "pretty," the blacks assure her, but also "stout," as if one's weight were a measure of one's beauty. Nor, in their view, should Mrs. Turpin regard the ugly girl's attack as a sign of God's judgment: "Jesus satisfied with her" they declare with wicked irony. Using a splendidly condescending qualifier that limits Ruby's supposed virtues to her own race, one of the Negro women declares that "I never knowed no sweeter white lady."

RUBY'S FINAL REFUGE

Mrs. Turpin is driven at last to her final refuge—to the pig "parlor" with its sanitation system so advanced that it makes her hogs cleaner than certain unkempt children. There she spies a huge pregnant sow lying on her side, grunting softly and panting with the new life teeming inside her. This image of animal innocence and contentment, because it contrasts so irksomely with her own guilt and turmoil, infuriates Ruby. She asks anyone who might be listening—chiefly God, of course—how she could be compared to such an ugly creature? "Why me?" she protests in splenetic self-defense. "It's no trash around here, black or white, that I haven't given to. And break my back to the bone every day working. And do for the church." Yet Ruby cannot forget the irksome fact that the ire of God broke not upon "niggers" or "trash" but upon this self-respecting woman who does not lie down in the middle of the street or "dip snuff and spit in every puddle and have it all over my chin." She is angry, above all, that God has not shown himself to be the Protector of white middle-class virtues that she had thought him to be.

None of her desperate self-justifications can calm Ruby Turpin's wrath. With the sky darkening into a deep bruised purple, she flings out her final taunt. Though God may overturn her idea of the social and moral hierarchy, putting the last first and making foolish the world's social wisdom, Ruby vows to keep clear the distinction between the bottom rail and the top. Again it is the humor of these scenes—unlike many of O'Connor's other judgment episodes—that is most notable. Ruby is indeed being painfully stripped of her confidence that the Lord helps those who help themselves and that cleanliness indicates godliness. Yet there is no fear that she will be overwhelmed by the loss. She is being forced, after all, to surrender what is not merely inessential but false.

Though her protests grow ever more profane—until finally she screams out, like an uninnocent Job, "Who do you think you are?"—they are also increasingly childish and futile. For the merest mortal sinner to demand that God account for his action is more silly than it is egregious. Sin is less cunning, O'Connor understands, than it is foolish. Thus is Ruby's arrogant query answered with an echo that turns the question back upon the questioner—as if God were asking *her,* "Who do you think you are?" This talky woman is left speechless at last. Like Nelson and Mr. Head, she is made to stand silent before a vision of purgatorial judgment that is also redeeming grace. It is imaged in the elongated purple cloud that arches above the lowering sun:

> She saw the streak as a vast swinging bridge extending upward from the earth through a field of living fire. Upon it was a vast horde of souls rumbling toward heaven. There were whole companies of white-trash, clean for the first time in their lives, and bands of black niggers in white robes, and battalions of freaks and lunatics [perhaps even Mary Grace] shouting and clapping and leaping like frogs. And bringing up the end of the procession was a tribe of people whom she recognized at once as those who, like herself and Claud, had always had a little of everything and the God-given wit to use it right. She leaned forward to observe them closer. They were marching behind the others with great dignity, accountable as they had always been for good order and common sense and respectable behavior. They alone were on key. Yet she could see by their shocked and altered faces that even their virtues were being burned away.

This passage is more powerful and convincing than the similar scene at the end of "The Artificial Nigger." Not only is it an affirmation visually rendered rather than discursively explained—"shown" rather than "told"—it is also a consummation that unites the entire story into a theological no less than a literary whole. Here, perhaps for the first time in O'Connor's fiction, divine wrath is couched wholly within the terms of divine mercy. It is a mercy that is like a refiner's fire—cleansing rather than consuming. Ruby Turpin's pride is purged by the flaming vision of all those "inferior" folk who are entering the Kingdom of God before her. O'Connor does not romantically exalt the poor and the outcast as intrinsically righteous. The down and out are God's favorites, compared to the clean and dignified Turpins of this world, simply because they are less bent on their own justification. Nor does O'Connor deny the importance of "good order and common sense and respectable behavior." Society could not exist without them. But because they often lead to spiritual arrogance, these very virtues become more pernicious than the common vices. Such spurious goodness must be burned away by the fires of God's grace.

TRUE FAITH IS INDELIBLE

The first and the last words of the Gospel are hopeful rather than baleful, and so are the beginning and the ending of this story. No one admitted entrance to purgatory can regress out of it. One's cleansing there may be greatly prolonged by one's own recalcitrant will, but there is no changing of direction, no going back on grace, no descent into hell from the precincts of mercy. However much they may differ about the doctrine of purgatory itself, classic Catholicism and classic Protestantism are here profoundly agreed: true faith is indelible and irreversible. Hence O'Connor's determination to embody, in this final scene of her finest story, the vision of an eschatological [relating to a branch of theology concerned with death and the ultimate destiny of mankind] community that includes all of the redeemed.

Ruby Turpin has no *rightful* place there. Yet, for all the horror of her sin, she is not driven out of the New Jerusalem and consigned to the realm of weeping and wailing and gnashing of teeth. She is given a glimpse, instead, of her own humble place in the economy of grace. This is cause not for lament but for rejoicing. So, as Ruby trudges home after the darkness has fallen and her vision has faded, she hears the sounds of jubilation rather than condemnation: "In the woods around her the invisible cricket choruses had struck up, but what she heard were the voices of the souls climbing into the starry field and shouting hallelujah." Ruby can hear this joyful noise not chiefly because she has met her own dreadful judgment, but because she has the prospect of being numbered among those singing souls. By God's grace alone, and not at all by her own good works, is her name written in the Lamb's Book of Life. Although she will surely not lead the roll, she has the comic and life-engendering hope of being least and last among all of God's children.

This, I submit, is the real comedy of our redemption. Flannery O'Connor is its superb artist and advocate because, in the best of her stories, she seeks not to wound but to heal, not to divide but to unite, not to shout but to jest, not to draw caricatures of damnation and salvation but to limn the subtleties and ironies of grace. This final concern with divine mercy explains her refusal to give the standard moralistic account of black-white relations. Only because God's justice is not primarily wrath but forgiveness can human injustice also be made redemptive rather than destructive. . . . Ruby Turpin is prepared to enter Paradise—and thus to live graciously in the quotidian world—because she has seen the gracious hierarchy of heaven.

A Critical Study of "A Good Man Is Hard to Find"

Miles Orvell

Miles Orvell is a professor of English and American
Studies at Temple University in Philadelphia. He is
the author of a variety of books about modern American culture, including *Invisible Parade: The Fiction
of Flannery O'Connor,* from which the following
article is excerpted. In it, Orvell offers a critical study
of O'Connor's most famous story "A Good Man Is
Hard to Find." He maintains that just before The
Misfit shoots and kills her, the grandmother—up until this point a foolish, racist, and self-righteous character—experiences a moment of grace when she
reaches out to touch The Misfit.

The epigraph to the collection *A Good Man Is Hard to Find*
reads: "The Dragon is by the side of the road, watching those
who pass. Beware lest he devour you. We go to the father of
souls, but it is necessary to pass by the dragon" (St. Cyril of
Jerusalem). It is especially fitting for the title story itself,
which begins by seeming, innocently enough, like a happy
journey from Atlanta to Florida; before it is over, however, a
dragon has not only materialized but has quite devoured the
entire traveling Bailey family. Yet Grandmother Bailey, at
least, seems to have gone on to "the father of souls." Her de-
liverer is an escaped convict who calls himself The Misfit.

The various members of the Bailey family are nicely indi-
vidualized, as to both physical and moral attributes: Bailey,
the pater familias, is an irritable, harassed, and stubborn
man, who doesn't "like to arrive at a motel with a cat." His
wife's face is "as broad and innocent as a cabbage," and she
ties around her head a green kerchief with "two points on

Excerpted from *Invisible Parade: The Fiction of Flannery O'Connor,* by Miles Orvell.
Copyright © 1991 by University Press of Mississippi. Reprinted with permission from
University Press of Mississippi.

the top like rabbit's ears." The couple's obnoxious children read comic books, fight among themselves, and are noticeably rude to strangers. But the story is focused on the grandmother, who—foolish, xenophobic, racially condescending, and self-righteously banal—is set off from the others in still more telling ways. Chiefly, she is the only one of the family who, in some way, expresses *care:* her personality moves outward toward others, toward the landscape, even toward her cat (significantly named Pitty Sing), whom she will not leave at home for fear he might accidentally turn on the gas and asphyxiate himself. And it is precisely this outward expression of care that will trigger The Misfit's cold rage.

THE GRANDMOTHER'S GRACIOUSNESS

One of the oblique signs of her grace, if we may prematurely call it such, is her graciousness, which O'Connor describes with her characteristically macabre humor: "Her collars and cuffs were white organdy trimmed with lace and at her neckline she had pinned a purple spray of cloth violets containing a sachet. In case of all accident, anyone seeing her dead on the highway would know at once that she was a lady." And she is somewhat prescient in this regard, for if she is not precisely dressed to kill, this remnant of Southern gentility is, as it turns out, dressed to be killed.

The plot device which sets in motion the confrontation with the intruding Misfit, is the travelers' diversion from the main road in search of a nice old mansion that the grandmother, remembering from the days of her youth, thinks is nearby. And there is a rightness about this search for the house that is not at first apparent. Significantly, the grandmother has been dozing off, and it is upon awakening, as if the splendid house had taken shape in her dreams, that she recalls it. An old plantation house, an idyllic memory of antebellum Southern life in all its imagined innocence and order, the image stands in sharp contrast to the depicted shabbiness of present-day life. And the old lady, in a successful effort to arouse the interest of the party, craftily embellishes her description by adding a secret panel, where the family silver was said to be hidden before Sherman's march.

What is barely concealed beneath the literal description of the mansion is its symbolic equivalence to a heavenly mansion; and the addition of the secret panel suggests its mysterious containment of the treasures of the past. It is home in the broadest sense—the place one starts out from, the place to which one returns. This favorite image of O'Connor's has already been noted in the homelier versions of Hazel Motes's Eastrod shack and the Powderhead cabin of the Tarwaters; and we have noted too the association of returning home with the image of the coffin (see "Judgement Day"); hence it is probably more than a merely accidental detail that Grandmother Bailey awakens from her nap at "Toombsboro" (the name of a real and desolate little town near Milledgeville, Georgia, by the way) to remember the mansion. What is suggested in these associations is a return, through death, to an earlier state of innocence and purity, to a place far off the main road, away from the sterility of the city, where one was a child, and to which one can return again only as a child. It may seem a small detail in a brutal image, but the woman's dying posture suggests her saving innocence: the killers look down "at the grandmother who half sat and half lay in a puddle of blood with her legs crossed under her like a child's and her face smiling up at the cloudless sky."

THE CHARACTER OF THE MISFIT

The agent of her death is of course The Misfit. No vulgar criminal, The Misfit, as his daddy said of him, is " 'a different breed of dog' " from his brothers and sisters; " 'it's some that can live their whole life out without asking about it and it's others has to know why it is, and this boy is one of the latters.' " Along with his metaphysical obsession (though the phrase sounds incongruous when applied to so homespun a character), The Misfit evinces a distinguishing gentility of manner, which the old lady, with her desperate equation of manners and morals, mistakes for goodness.

As The Misfit's co-disaffiliates (they, however, are just "common") proceed to murder the Bailey family, the lingering grandmother engages the escaped convict in a revealing dialogue. And in The Misfit's accented account of his past, O'Connor mixes just the right elements of classic American drifter and morbid sophisticate to lend credibility and authority to an essentially enigmatic figure. " 'I was a gospel singer for a while. . . . Been in the arm service . . . been twict married, been an undertaker, been with the railroads, plowed Mother Earth, been in a tornado, seen a man burnt alive oncet. . . . I even seen a woman flogged.' " At the root of

The Misfit's meanness, however, are not these experiences but a cosmic sense of injustice—of a universe out of kilter: "'I call myself The Misfit . . . because I can't make what all I done wrong fit what all I gone through in punishment [he has escaped from a penitentiary].'" And the paragon of all who are wronged is, for The Misfit, Jesus. And yet, what complicates his problem vastly is precisely the grander aspects of Jesus: '[Jesus] thown everything off balance. If He did what He said [raise the dead], then it's nothing for you to do but thow away everything and follow Him, and if He didn't, then it's nothing for you to do but enjoy the few minutes you got left the best way you can—by killing somebody or burning down his house or doing some other meanness to him. No pleasure but meanness,' he said and his voice had become almost a snarl."

It is a violent logic, and it draws so sharp a line between the total commitment of faith and the total commitment of disbelief that there is no middle course. Moreover, it is the same logic that applied to Hazel Motes in his career and that we have seen exemplified in what would be the later conflict between the principles of old Tarwater and those of the devil. The middle way—the way of humanism (for example, Rayber)—is, for O'Connor, the way of self-deception and self-destruction. Unless we understand the argument, we are likely to misread The Misfit as an equally perverse logician and theologian. Such is not the case, however, for if he is diabolically misguided in his inexorable commitment to his logic, the logic of his commitment is, for O'Connor, itself inexorable.

Put another way, what The Misfit lacks (and what Hazel and Tarwater, for example, are given) is a vision of grace: and, nostalgically, he yearns for just that; but the language in which he phrases his desire points to his implicit denial of the ongoing action of mercy, and, instead, fixes the redemptive act (Jesus' raising of the dead) in a single historical moment of time. "'It ain't right I wasn't there because if I had of been there I would of known. Listen lady,' he said in a high voice, 'if I had of been there I would of known and I wouldn't be like I am now.'" It is at this point, the moment of his confessed privation from grace, that the grandmother is given *her* moment of grace. "She saw the man's face twisted close to her own as if he were going to cry and she murmured, 'Why you're one of my babies. You're one of my own children!'"

Though he has taken her dead son Bailey's shirt, The Misfit is unwilling to acquiesce in the proffered adoption. In her last gesture of gracious care toward the world, the old lady reaches out to touch him on the shoulder. "The Misfit sprang back as if a snake had bitten him and shot her three times through the chest." For the old lady's gesture, like Christ's, throws everything off balance, and it is perceived by The Misfit, ironically, as the Snake's temptation. His own act, then, of shooting the woman, is conceived by him, one imagines, as a reestablishment of the particular order of his own world. That, perhaps, is the meaning of his deadpan reply to his henchman Bobby Lee's question following the shooting, and it must strike the reader as at once logically inescapable and yet, with the extravagance of the iterative image, grimly humorous.

> "She was a talker, wasn't she?" Bobby Lee said, sliding down the ditch with a yodel.
>
> "She would of been a good woman," The Misfit said, " if it had been somebody there to shoot her every minute of her life."
>
> "Some fun!" Bobby Lee said.
>
> "Shut up, Bobby Lee," The Misfit said. "It's no real pleasure in life."

But there is perhaps the seed of a new dissatisfaction in those last words of his, which deny what he had earlier affirmed ("No pleasure but meanness"). O'Connor's own comment on the conclusion carries forward the suggestion. "I don't want to equate The Misfit with the devil. I prefer to think that, however unlikely this may seem, the old lady's gesture, like the mustard-seed, will grow to be a great crow-filled tree in The Misfit's heart, and will be enough of a pain to him there to turn him into the prophet he was meant to become. But that's another story."

THE OVERALL EFFECT OF "A GOOD MAN IS HARD TO FIND"

It is difficult to define the effect of a story like "A Good Man Is Hard to Find." We have been moved by an invisible narrative hand, from a gently satirical fiction with interesting shades of local color to a brutal confrontation that, while it ends with a massacre of innocents, yet does not permit us to sentimentalize their deaths (indeed the grandmother's death strangely elevates her)—but rather draws our attention to the figure of the killer, who is himself no vicious creation, but a comic character. And one cannot separate the effect of such a story from its style, so that, as Elizabeth Hardwick aptly put it, "You'll have to call *A Good Man Is Hard to Find* a 'funny' story even though six people are killed in it." For the brutality and cruelty of The Misfit are carefully kept under control by the detachment of the narrative and the abstract logic of the drama. And yet, there is no denying "the puddle of blood" the old lady is left lying in.

A Contrasting View of "A Good Man Is Hard to Find"

Stephen C. Bandy

In the article that follows, literary critic Stephen C. Bandy offers an alternative reading of O'Connor's "A Good Man Is Hard to Find." In contrast to the view of most literary critics—and the author herself—that the grandmother's final actions reflect a moment of grace, Bandy asserts that the grandmother remains selfish and immoral throughout the entire story. When the grandmother says to The Misfit, "Why you're one of my babies. You're one of my own children!," she is resorting to her only remaining weapon—motherhood—as a way to convince him to spare her life. Bandy is a professor of English at Pace University in New York City.

Criticism of Flannery O'Connor's fiction, under the spell of the writer's occasional comments, has been unusually susceptible to interpretations based on Christian dogma. None of O'Connor's stories has been more energetically theologized than her most popular, "A Good Man Is Hard To Find." O'Connor flatly declared the story to be a parable of grace and redemption, and for the true believer there can be no further discussion. As James Mellard remarks, "O'Connor simply tells her readers—either through narrative interventions or be extra-textual exhortations—how they are to interpret her work." And should not the writer know best what her story is about? A loaded question, to which the best answer may be D.H. Lawrence's advice: trust the art, but not the artist.

One cannot deny that the concerns of this story are the basic concerns of Christian belief: faith, death, salvation. And

Excerpted from "One of My Babies: The Misfit and the Grandmother," by Stephen C. Bandy, *Studies in Short Fiction*, Winter 1996. Copyright © 1996 by Newberry College. Reprinted with permission.

yet, if one reads the story without prejudice, there would seem to be little here to inspire hope for redemption of any of its characters. No wishful search for evidence of grace or for epiphanies of salvation, by author or reader, can soften the harsh truth of "A Good Man Is Hard To Find." Its message is profoundly pessimistic and in fact subversive to the doctrines of grace and charity, despite heroic efforts to disguise that fact. This vexing little masterpiece cannot be saved from itself. It has a will of its own and a moral of its own.

There are really only two characters in this story: the Grandmother and the Misfit. The rest are wonderfully drawn—hateful little June Star, or whiny Red Sammy—but they do not figure in the central debate. Although the Misfit is not physically present until the final pages, his influence hangs over the story almost from the beginning, when the Grandmother warns her son Bailey of the dangerous criminal "aloose from the Federal Pen." Once the family sets off on their vacation trip, the Grandmother seems to forget her feigned concern, for it is only a strategy by which she hopes to force Bailey to take the family in another direction. But the reader has not forgotten. We wonder only when, and where, the inevitable confrontation will take place. At Red Sam's filling station, we suppose. But O'Connor has other plans, which are fulfilled in a chain of events so contrived, so improbable, and so perfectly appropriate to this carful of cartoon characters, that we can only be delighted by the writer's disdain for the niceties of plotting. It is a brilliant stroke: their car rolls over in a field miles from anywhere; and then, as sure as sundown, the Misfit and his crew slowly move toward them. The story rapidly moves to its climax, when the Misfit shoots the Grandmother dead. But what comes just before that killing interests us even more. The Misfit has already directed the execution of the Grandmother's entire family, and it must be obvious to all, including reader and Grandmother, that she is the next to die. But she struggles on. Grasping at any appeal, and hardly aware of what she is saying, the Grandmother declares to the Misfit: "Why you're one of my babies. You're one of my own children!" As she utters these shocking words, "She reached out and touched him on the shoulder. The Misfit sprang back as if a snake had bitten him and shot her three times through the chest."

Noting that some squeamish readers had found this ending too strong, O'Connor defended the scene in this way: "If I took out this gesture and what she says with it, I would have no story. What was left would not be worth your attention." Certainly the scene is crucial to the story, and most readers, I think, grant its dramatic "rightness" as a conclusion. What is arguable is the meaning to the Grandmother's final words to the Misfit, as well as her "gesture," which seemed equally important to O'Connor. One's interpretation depends on one's opinion of the Grandmother.

THE GRANDMOTHER'S CHARACTER

What are we to think of this woman? At the story's beginning, she seems a harmless busybody, utterly self-absorbed but also amusing, in her way. And, in her way, she provides a sort of human Rorschach test of her readers. We readily forgive her so much, including her mindless racism—she points at the "cute little pickaninny" by the roadside, and entertains her grandchildren with a story in which a watermelon is devoured by "a nigger boy." She is filled with the prejudices of her class and her time. And so, some readers conclude, she is in spite of it all a "good" person. Somewhat more ominously, the Misfit—after he has fired three bullets into her chest—pronounces that she might have been "a good woman . . . if it had been somebody there to shoot her every minute of her life." We surmise that in the universe of this story, the quality of what is "good" (which is after all the key word of the story's title) depends greatly on who is using the term. I do not think the Misfit is capable of irony—he truly means what he says about her, even though he finds it necessary to kill her. Indeed, the opposing categories of "good" and "evil" are very much in the air throughout this story. But like most supposed opposites, they have an alarming tendency to merge. It is probably worth noting that the second line of the once-popular song that gave O'Connor her title is "You always get the other kind."

Much criticism of the story appears to take a sentimental view of the Grandmother largely because she is a grandmother. Flannery O'Connor herself, as we shall see shortly, found little to blame in this woman, choosing to wrap her in the comfortable mantle of elderly Southern womanhood. O'Connor applies this generalization so uncritically that we half suspect she is pulling our leg. In any case, we can be sure that such sentimentality (in the mind of either the writer or her character) is fatal to clear thinking. If the Grandmother is old (although she does not seem to be that old), grey-haired, and "respectable," it follows that she must be weak, gentle, and benevolent—precisely the Grandmother's opinion of herself, and she is not shy of letting others know it. Intentionally or not, O'Connor has etched the Grandmother's character with wicked irony, which makes it all the more surprising to read the author's response to a frustrated teacher whose (Southern) students persisted in favoring the Grandmother, despite his strenuous efforts to point out her flaws. O'Connor said, "I had to tell him that they resisted ... because they all had grandmothers or great-aunts just like her at home, and they knew, from personal experience, that the old lady lacked comprehension, but that she had a good heart."

O'Connor continued, "The Southerner is usually tolerant of those weaknesses that proceed from innocence, and he knows that a taste for self-preservation can be readily combined with the missionary spirit." What is most disappointing in this moral summary of the Grandmother, and her ilk, is its disservice to the spiky, vindictive woman of the story. There may be a purpose to O'Connor's betrayal of her own character: her phrase "missionary spirit" gives the game away. O'Connor is determined that the Grandmother shall be the Misfit's savior, even though she may not seem so in the story.

The Grandmother's role as grace-bringer is by now a received idea, largely because the author said it is so. But one must question the propriety of such tinkering with the character, after the fact. It reduces the firebreathing woman who animates this story to nothing much more than a cranky maiden aunt. On the contrary, the Grandmother is a fierce fighter, never more so than in her final moments, nose-to-nose with the Misfit. Granted, the Grandmother is not a homicidal monster like the Misfit, and she certainly does not deserve to die for her minor sins. And yet, does she quite earn absolution from any moral weakness beyond that of "a hypocritical old soul"? For every reader who sees the image of his or her own grandmother printed on this character's cold face, as O'Connor suggested we might do, there are surely many others who can only be appalled by a calculating opportunist who is capable of embracing her family's murderer, to save her own skin. Where indeed is the "good heart" which unites this unprincipled woman with all those "grandmothers or great-aunts just like her at home"? The answer to that question can only be an affirmation of the "banality of evil," to use Hannah Arendt's well-known phrase.

O'Connor did not exactly defend the Grandmother's selfish behavior; but the writer famously described this final gesture as "the action of grace in the Grandmother's soul." Following O'Connor's suggestion, other commentators have elaborated upon the doctrine of grace as it might appear in this episode, sometimes with surprising results: Robert H. Brinkmeyer urges, "No longer just a silly old lady, she reaches out in a Christ-like gesture to touch the Misfit, declaring he is one of her children."

The doctrine of grace has caused endless trouble in the historic theological debates of the Church. Grace is not to be invoked lightly, particularly in a secular milieu. Even now there is no settled interpretation; through the centuries the Church has entertained a variety of views regarding the mechanics of grace. To bring the complex machinery of this theological abstraction into the alien world of the Grandmother and the Misfit is more than inappropriate. It is inapplicable. What does in fact happen in this part of the story is quite straightforward: the Grandmother, having exhausted all other appeals to the Misfit, resorts to her only remaining (though certainly imperfect) weapon: motherhood. Declaring to the Misfit that he is one of her babies, she sets out to conquer him. Perhaps she hopes that this ultimate flattery will melt his heart, and he will collapse in her comforting motherly embrace. Such are the stratagems of sentimentality. The moral shoddiness of her action is almost beyond description. If we had not already guessed the depths to which the Grandmother might sink, now we know. It is not easy to say who is the more evil, the Misfit or the Grandmother, and indeed that is the point. Her behavior is the manifest of her character.

It has been said that no action is without its redeeming aspect. Could this unspeakable act of selfishness carry within it the seeds of grace, acting, as it were, above the Grandmother? So Flannery O'Connor believed. But what is the precise movement of grace in this scene? It is surely straining the text to propose that the Grandmother has in this moment "seen the light." Are we to regard her as the unwitting agent of divine grace whose selfish intentions are somehow transfigured into a blessing? Such seems to have been O'Connor's opinion: ". . . however unlikely this may seem, the old lady's gesture, like the mustard-seed, will grow to be a great crow-filled tree in the Misfit's heart, and will be enough of a pain to him there to turn him into the prophet he was meant to become." We are almost persuaded to forget that none of this happens in the story itself. If this can be so, then we can just as easily attribute any interpretation we like to the scene. But in fact he is in no way changed. There is no "later on" in fiction. We do not, and will not, see "created grace" in the spirit of the Misfit. . . .

In this light, to describe the Grandmother as the vessel of divine grace, almost in spite of herself, is to transform her into a creature who simply has nothing to do with the Grandmother's character, as given. In dismissing O'Connor's claims of this moment of grace, Satterfield rightly observes that "when the author made such statements—and she made plenty of them—she was speaking as a propagandist, not an artist." It is a purely intellectual conceit, which in a real sense betrays her integrity as a character. At the risk of repeating myself, this interpretation can be valid only if it is intrinsic to the story, and not imposed upon the story. (A useful contrast can be made with O'Connor's "Revelation," in which the final hallucination, or revelation, of Mrs. Turpin surely qualifies as an experience of unmistakable sacramental significance.)

THE GRANDMOTHER'S PRINCIPLE OF "BY ANY MEANS NECESSARY"

At her moment of extremity, the Grandmother lurches desperately from one strategy to another, not quite admitting to herself that the Misfit will kill her just as casually as he has killed the rest of her family. All of her ruses, so dependable in the past, have failed. We are well acquainted with her manipulative techniques: her fruitless deceptions of her son Bailey (who knows her little games too well to be fooled), or her shameless pandering to the gas station's "Red Sammy," whom she assures, in the automatic way of habitual flatterer, that he is indeed a "good man"—a casual tossing-off of the phrase that will at the last seal her fate, when she uses it once too often. The Grandmother has perfected the technique of the insincere compliment, and we suppose that she has used it to great effect for most of her life. But not this time. The Misfit, withdrawing ever deeper into the dank recesses of his memories, hardly seems to hear her words, or even to notice her, until she mentions Jesus. And then, misjudging his reaction, she makes the great mistake of reaching out to touch him.

Here as elsewhere, the Grandmother's guiding principle seems to be "by any means necessary." As was mentioned earlier, in our first view of the Grandmother we witness a chilling demonstration of her selfishness. She is determined to coerce her son to take the family on vacation to Tennessee rather than Florida. To accomplish this end, she does not hesitate to dangle before his eyes the horrifying prospect of his children's death:

"Now look here, Bailey," she said, "see here, read this," and she stood with one hand on her thin hip and the other rattling the newspaper at his bald head. "Here this fellow that calls himself The Misfit is aloose from the Federal Pen and headed toward Florida and you read here what it says he did to these people. Just you read it. I wouldn't take my children in any direction with a criminal like that aloose in it. I couldn't answer to my conscience if I did."

Bailey is unmoved. He has heard such idle threats from his mother all his life. But at the story's end, in a possibly too perfect irony, her prediction comes true, as the result of her meddling. The sting in the tail of this irony is that they would never have met the Misfit at all, if Bailey had given in to the Grandmother's demand to go to Tennessee, instead of Florida. To be sure, this is fore-shadowing with a vengeance.

The Grandmother's petty acts of deception are, it seems at first glance, merely that—petty acts. Profoundly dishonest, she stops at nothing to have her way. Against Bailey's orders, she has smuggled her cat (Pitty Sing by name, an allusion to The Mikado that may reflect the Grandmother's less apparent cultural aspirations) aboard the car as they begin their trip. Much later, the cat's leaping onto Bailey's back will cause the accident that leads directly into the final scenes of the story. (Anyone who has traveled long distances with a cat might marvel at the fact that Pitty Sing has managed to remain in her basket undetected all this time.) As the family sets out, the Grandmother puts on her public face: carefully turned out in a lace-trimmed dress, straw sailor hat, and a sachet pinned at the neckline, so that "In case of an accident, anyone seeing her dead on the highway would know at once that she was a lady."

Her vanity is remarkable. But the Grandmother prefers to see herself as a valiant defender of social decorum in a world of barbarians. She speaks often and at length of the decline of civility, which in her lexicon seems a synonym for obedience—of the lack of trust, lack of respect (especially for her), and of the sad fact that people are "not nice like they used to be." At the same time, she herself trusts no one and has respect for no one who gets in her way. She is in fact a woman with neither values nor morals, though she would be shocked to be told so.

But what of it? What harm finally comes of her simple-minded preoccupation with herself? The answer to that question, it seems to me, is the key to this story, and it becomes clear only when she is face-to-face with the Misfit. He too is a person who lives only for himself, yet knowing that (as he angrily chastises the uncomprehending Bobby Lee) "It's no real pleasure in life." But the Misfit has at least this advantage over the Grandmother: he knows who he is. And worse for her, he knows who she is.

In her efforts to strike a soft place in the heart of the Misfit, the Grandmother leads their conversation into religious channels. That is, she admonishes him to "pray," perhaps hoping to distract him from the frightening recital of his violent life: "If you would pray . . . Jesus would help you." Mentioning the name of Jesus is a mistake, for it ignites a slow-burning fuse in the mind of the Misfit. It seems that he has given Jesus a good deal of thought—far more than the Grandmother ever had done. Indeed, as she continues to mutter the name of Jesus, "the way she was saying it, it sounded as if she might be cursing." With cold intensity, never raising his voice, the Misfit intones, "Jesus thown everything off balance. It was the same case with Him as with me except He hadn't committed any crime. . . ." Ignoring the Grandmother's wailing, the Misfit pursues his obsession: "Jesus was the only One that ever raised the dead . . . and He shouldn't have done it. He thown everything off balance." For the Misfit, as for many others (including Jesus himself on the cross), the problem is one of faith. He cannot believe, because he has no proof. Therefore, the choice is clear:

"If He did what He said, then it's nothing for you to do but throw away everything and follow Him, and if He didn't, then it's nothing for you to do but enjoy the few minutes you got left the best way you can—by killing somebody or burning down his house or doing some other meanness to him. No pleasure but meanness," he said and his voice had become almost a snarl.

This is the Misfit's philosophy of life—nasty, short, and brutish. Crude and inarticulate though it be, the Misfit's view of life has an ancient pedigree, linking him to the original Sinner himself. Like Milton's Satan, he lives by the creed, "Evil, be thou my good!" The sin of Satan, according to Milton, echoing the words of the Fathers of the Church from St. Augustine onward, was superbia, the monstrous pride that begets all other sins. But the heavenstorming defiance of the Archfiend is diminished, just as the underpinnings of theology have gradually fallen away. The non serviam of Satan becomes merely the sour nihilism of the Misfit. His anger has nothing to do with the yearning for freedom that makes Milton's Satan such a curiously sympathetic character. The Misfit's anger is the product of a conviction that nothing has value, not even freedom. No pleasure but meanness.

The emptiness in the soul of the Misfit is not an absence of religious faith (as the Grandmother naively sees it), but his lack of any kind of faith at all. The Misfit trusts nothing that he has not himself witnessed, touched, weighed and measured. This is his "reality." Whatever transcends that reality—faith, hope, and charity might sum it up very well—has no meaning for him. He will not trust the miracles of Jesus because, as he agitatedly complains to the Grandmother, "It ain't right I wasn't there because if I had of been there I would of known." The Misfit's inability to believe has destroyed his humanity. His nihilism is complete: "No pleasure but meanness.". . .

ONE OF THE BABIES

Unlike the Grandmother, the Misfit has struggled to understand good and evil. His final verdict is relentlessly logical. And yet, surprisingly, their philosophical positions—his by determination, hers by accident—are not so far apart in the end. By his lights, she could have been "a good woman"—if only she had not talked so much. Traveling by two different routes, the Grandmother and the Misfit have arrived at the same destination, both geographically and intellectually. No words could be more shocking, and yet appropriate: "Why you're one of my babies. You're one of my own children!" Indeed he is one of her babies; for her lack of values is his lack as well. Those two faces, so close together, are mirror images. The Misfit is simply a more completely evolved form of the Grandmother. In truth, one of her babies.

To insist at this moment of mutual revelation that the Grandmother is transformed into the agent of God's grace is to do serious violence to the story. It is as tendentious as to decree that the three bullets in her chest symbolize the Trinity. At the end, "A Good Man is Hard to Find" descends further into the depths of existential despair than very many other examples of twentieth-century fiction: Celine perhaps, or among American writers, Henry Miller. There is a fierce internal coherence to the character of the Grandmother, and it has nothing to do with forgiveness, witting or unwitting. Flannery O'Connor built better than she knew—or at any rate, better than she dared acknowledge.

Prophecy in "The Displaced Person"

Kathleen Feeley

Sister Kathleen Feeley, former president of the College of Notre Dame of Maryland, currently acts as the director of special education for the Baltimore city schools. In the subsequent article, excerpted from her book *Flannery O'Connor: Voice of the Peacock,* Feeley examines the role of prophecy in "The Displaced Person." She contends that the story contains two prophets: Mrs. Shortly, a false prophet motivated by fear and ignorance, and Mr. Guizac, a true prophet who evinces trust and innocence.

In "The Displaced Person," one sees evidence of the kind of prophecy that O'Connor attributed to the novelist:

> The writer's gaze has to extend beyond the surface, beyond mere problems, until it touches the realm of mystery which is the concern of prophets. True prophecy in the novelist's case is a matter of seeing near things with their extensions of meaning and thus of seeing far things close up.

The "near" situation which this story explores is the disruption of normal farm and social life which a displaced person from Poland, Mr. Guizac, causes at Mrs. McIntyre's farm. Mechanically inclined, hard-working, and thrifty, he brings such new prosperity to the farm that Mrs. McIntyre exclaims with gratitude, "That man is my salvation!" But he displays a single-mindedness in the work which must be done; he does not adjust to the lazy, thieving ways of the Negroes nor condone the slovenly habits of the white dairyman, Mr. Shortley. He does not speak the language of his new country nor understand its social customs. Eventually the prosperity which he brings to the farm has its own price: the Shortleys leave to keep from being fired; Mrs. Shortley dies from a heart attack caused by their sudden departure; and the Negroes become sullen. Mrs. McIntyre herself turns against the

Pole when she learns that he has promised his sixteen-year-old cousin in marriage to Sulk, a half-witted Negro, if Sulk pays half of her fare from the refugee camp in which she has been living. When she discovers this arrangement, Mrs. McIntyre is convinced that the man whom she termed a "miracle" has turned into a "monster." From that time on, her perspective changes. Mr. Guizac's virtues become faults. She wants desperately to get rid of him, but lacks the courage to fire him. On a chill autumn day, she and Mr. Shortley and Sulk watch the displaced person as he lies on the ground fixing a machine; they fail to warn him that the brake on a nearby tractor has slipped, and the three, with a look "that froze them in collusion forever," watch the tractor crush him to death.

Such is the "near" situation. That it will have "extensions of meaning" is indicated by the description of the peacock which opens the story. The peacock's tail, "glittering green-gold and blue in the sunlight . . . flowed out on either side like a floating train and his head on the long blue reed-like neck was drawn back as if his attention were fixed in the distance on something no one else could see." Throughout the story the displaced person suggests the divine displacement, the Incarnation; and the peacock suggests the glory of spiritual reality. In a perceptive analysis of this story, Robert Fitzgerald says of the peacock: "An unpredictable splendor, a map of the universe, doted upon by the priest, barely seen by everyone else: this is a metaphor, surely, for God's order and God's grace." One is tempted to make a direct analogy between the story and its significance, but Flannery O'Connor does not write allegory. She calls herself "a realist of distances," and she displays that realism here. In its extended meaning, "The Displaced Person" suggests man's alienation from his true country—the supernatural realm; symbolically the story unites the historical coming of Christ in his humanity and his final coming in glory at the end of time.

This union is suggested in a scene in which the priest who arranged for the Guizac family to come to America is listening to Mrs. McIntyre's complaints about the displaced person. Just as the unpleasant conversation is ending, the priest sees the peacock. Gazing at the "tiers of small pregnant suns float[ing] in a green-gold haze," the priest murmurs, "Christ will come like that," as he envisions the glory of Christ's coming at the end of time. Then, seconds later, he murmurs, "the Transfiguration," recalling the scriptural account of Christ's being transfigured in glory once during his earthly life. While his mind is filled with Christ's glorification, Mrs. McIntyre has been defending her intention to dismiss Mr. Guizac. As the cock lowers his tail, she repeats her previous sentence about the displaced person: "He didn't have to come in the first place." Still caught up in his own thoughts, the priest's mind moves from the glory of Christ's divinity to the grace of his humanity, and he replies, "He came to redeem us."

THE TWO PROPHETS IN "THE DISPLACED PERSON"

There are two prophets in this story, which pits the laws of the countryside against the precepts of the "true country," and each prophet is overtaken suddenly by death. Mrs. Shortley, the "giant wife of the countryside," suffers a fatal heart attack; Mr. Guizac is, in effect, murdered by his employer and her two farm hands. The first, goaded by fear and ignorance, makes herself into a prophet; the second, living in trust and innocence, becomes an unwitting prophet.

Mrs. Shortley, who dies in the first part of this tripartite story, becomes Mr. Guizac's chief foe. She truly believes he is diabolical because she cannot countenance what she cannot understand. As soon as she sees him bow from the waist and kiss Mrs. McIntyre's hand, she distrusts him. In her thoughts, she connects him with the "Europe" which the newsreels have shown her: a mysterious "devil's experiment station" typified by "a small room piled high with bodies of dead naked people all in a heap, their arms and legs tangled together, a head thrust in here, a head there, a foot, a knee, a part that should have been covered up sticking out, a hand raised clutching nothing." Looking with unseeing eyes at the peacock in the tree in front of her, its tail like "a map of the universe," she experiences an "inner vision" of millions of D.P.'s replacing all the Negro farm hands. She is afraid of all foreigners, "people who were all eyes and no understanding," people whose religion had not been reformed. In fact, this "unreformed" religion becomes the basis of her fear. She pictures the priest as an emissary of the devil, perhaps the devil himself. Fear of the unknown drives her to her Bible. "She pored over the Apocalypse and began to quote from the Prophets" and before long she has a vision, born of ignorance. (The description of her exertion while climbing a steep incline to drive home the cows indicates that her "vision" is actually a minor heart attack.) With her eyes closed she sees a blood-red figure with spinning white wheels, and she hears a voice say, "Prophesy." In a comic parody of the warnings of the Old Testament prophets, she cries in a loud voice, "The children of wicked nations will be butchered. Legs where arms should be, foot to face, ear in palm of hand. Who will remain whole? Who will remain whole? Who?" This prophecy is related to her final heart attack. As the Shortleys drive away from the farm, her vision seems to reverse itself, as if she is "looking inside" herself. She grasps her husband's elbow and her daughter's foot "as if she were trying to fit the two extra limbs onto herself." Her eyes, forced closed during her "vision," are open in death "to contemplate for the first time the tremendous frontiers of her true country."

A false prophet wedded to the countryside, Mrs. Shortley finds her "true country" in death; a true prophet whose life is conformed to spiritual reality, Mr. Guizac abides in his true country. The displaced person does not prophesy; in fact, he hardly speaks in the story. Yet he is a true prophet, one of the men "who challenge the disorder of the surrounding society with the order they experience as living in themselves," to use [philosopher Eric] Voegelin's definition. Mr. Guizac evokes the hostility of the people around him because he orders his life to a reality which they cannot grasp. As Mrs. McIntyre says, "He's upset the balance around here." Only at his death does Mrs. McIntyre realize that the center of balance might not be herself. She watches the figures bending over Mr. Guizac's body—the priest, his wife, and his two children. She hears the priest murmur words that she doesn't understand and sees him put something into the crushed man's mouth. Dimly aware of an invisible reality, she "felt she was in some foreign country where the people bent over the body were natives, and she watched like a stranger while the dead man was carried away in the ambulance."

MAN'S RELATIONSHIP TO REALITY

The "extensions of meaning" in this story include most of Flannery O'Connor's ideas about man's relationship to reality. . . . Both Mrs. Shortley and her husband falsify their own natures. Mrs. Shortley becomes a false prophet because she fears the mysterious reality which the displaced person has introduced into her secure world; her husband makes himself an arm of the Lord to avenge his wife's death, for which he blames the displaced person. Mrs. McIntyre is so concerned over the prosperity of her farm that she alienates herself from any other reality. As far as she is concerned, "Christ is just another D.P." She listens to the priest's talk about "when God sent his Only Begotten Son" with impatience, and finally interrupts with the statement, "I want to talk to you about something serious." The death of the displaced person has a historical and social significance as deep as its religious one. The death-dealing conflict between the European "old world" with its unreformed religion and quaint social customs and the new, brash, pragmatic American world is epitomized in the death of Mr. Guizac at the hands of a resentful white farm laborer, a sullen Negro, and a fear-filled landowner, all of whom share an intuition that the foreigner is likely to displace them. Father Flynn is childlike in his attention to reality. For him, its numinous quality is immediately evident. As soon as he arrives at the farm, he is entranced by the glory of the peacock, even with its splendid tail folded. The old priest "crept forward on tiptoe and looked down on the bird's back where the polished gold and green design began." Whenever he visits the farm he seems to have two objects in mind: to speak of spiritual reality to Mrs. McIntyre, and to see it in the natural world around him. Mrs. Shortley notices that he goes about "picking up feathers off the ground." One time, finding "two peacock feathers and four or five turkey feathers and an old brown hen feather," he "took them off with him like a bouquet"—a reminder of the grandeur with which the world is charged. Mr. Guizac, more a "presence" than an actor in the story, is a prophet who carries with him the aura of his native country, Christianity. In "The Displaced Person," one thus sees in microcosm all of Flannery O'Connor's main themes.

That this one story contains so many O'Connor themes is both a sign of Flannery's artistry and an indication of the unity of her vision of natural and supernatural reality. She explored these same themes, concentrating on one and then another, in all her fiction. From a comment in a letter to a friend, written late in her short life, she seems to have realized that she had developed these themes as extensively as she could. With her clear gaze turned toward herself, she wrote to Sister Mariella Gable, "I've been writing for eighteen years and I've reached the point where I can't do again what I know I can do well, and the larger things that I need to do now, I doubt my capacity for doing." Fourteen months later she was dead.

John Ciardi has said that a man is finally defined by what he gives his attention to. During her years of writing, Flannery O'Connor gave her attention to the visible world around her, and the spiritual life that permeates it. She said once that writing was a terrible experience (adding, cryptically, "You never know if you will finish it or it will finish you"). "Terrible," too, is the fiction which she wrote. Her stories cause terror or fear; they are dreadful; they elicit awe; they are extreme in degree; they are intense, severe, excessive. Only art could make such fiction beautiful; only reality could sustain such intense art. Only an artist penetrated with Christianity could use such extreme means to evoke from reality its full measure of splendor.

"Parker's Back": The Transformation of an Unbeliever

Richard Giannone

Many critics consider "Parker's Back" to be O'Connor's most comic story—in large part due to the character of O.E. Parker, who at fourteen was so awestruck by a tattooed performer at a fair that he grows obsessed with getting tattoos. In the selection that follows, excerpted from his book *Flannery O'Connor and the Mystery of Love*, Richard Giannone maintains that Parker's final tattoo—a Byzantine Christ on his back—signifies his transformation from a lazy and irresponsible womanizer to a man who finds union with God. Giannone is a professor of modern American literature at Fordham University, a Jesuit university in New York City.

A vision with a message comes twice to O.E. Parker in "Parker's Back" during his twenty-eight years. The first comes when he is fourteen and neatly divides his history in half. At a fair he sees a sideshow performer tattooed from head to foot with pictures that jump alive as the man flexes his muscles. Drawings of people and animals and flowers move as a single intricate dance of creation before the gaping young hero. The next fourteen years become a search for the awe Parker felt at the fair. His quest for excitation ends, as it began, with a vision. Parker is operating a tractor that crashes into an enormous tree; on impact, his shoes and the tree and the tractor burst into a Mosaic theophany so intense that Parker feels the fiery breath of the burning tree on his face.

The biblical character of these visions escapes Parker. Religion is useless to him. Rugged confidence in himself requires that he dismiss any thought of divine influence. "'A man can't save his self from whatever it is he don't deserve none of my sympathy,'" he says to the tattooist, who asks Parker if he is saved. Parker's disregard for religion exists side by side with his powerful sense of mystery. The vivid concreteness of the performer's tattoos and the scorching picture of the burning tree stir him to act and search and feel in new ways. He grasps their emotional force with clarity while remaining baffled by what, if anything, they mean to him.

To a person of faith, everything is miraculous insofar as it is touched by the hand of God, but the unbeliever must sort things out by her or his own devices. "Parker's Back," like *Wise Blood*, has an accidental vision throw the hero for a loop so that he can go back through his personal negations to the source of power that arouses him in the first place. Like Hazel Motes, O.E. Parker responds to an indomitable presence with his full being. He habitually stands before the world with his mouth hanging open. When he joins the navy, his mouth closes; but five years of naval hardening no more stamp out Parker's desire for ecstatic excitement than a four-year hitch in the army alters Hazel's decision to avoid Jesus. Life on a drab mechanical ship cannot dim Parker's oceanic eyes, which reflect in miniature the immense "mysterious sea." He is spiritual without being religious. Astonishment remains Parker's talent, and his capacity for wonderment in the physical world leads him to God.

Parker's sensuality assists him in his movement Godward. He likes his women fleshy, amiable, and numerous. His adolescent delight in tattoos serves his manly pleasure with women, since he "had never yet met a woman who was not attracted to them." Yet beneath his swelling ego, there lies the nagging sense of feeling ordinary. This unformed feeling disposes Parker to the aggressive female, who can direct and shape his desire. When his truck breaks down on the highway, he meets Sarah Ruth Cates, who is skinny and bossy and indifferent enough to his sexual stance that he marries her to meet the challenge of her libidinal coldness. Parker is another Chantecleer whose favorite is a henpecking Pertelote. Sarah Ruth is to the core the strict, God-fearing daughter of a Straight Gospel preacher. Try as he may, Parker cannot get Sarah Ruth's approval, even though her pregnancy suggests that her body and heart have not totally surrendered to her mind. The hero's last and desperate attempt to break through her rigidity takes the form of having a Byzantine Christ tattooed on his back. Instead of winning Sarah Ruth over, the tattooed Christ becomes another vision, the decisive one. This vision embeds into Parker's body and spirit the message seen but vaguely understood on the performer's body and in the burning tree.

PARKER'S SEARCH FOR DISCIPLINE

Without Sarah Ruth, Parker could not decipher what is on his back and what comes before his eyes in the tree. Marriage sharpens his ambivalent feelings about himself and the world into creative opposition to the drabness around him. If he is "puzzled and ashamed of himself" for staying with his ruthless wife, Parker also seeks out the very discipline that Sarah Ruth embodies. Her gray eyes that are sharpened into two icepicks resemble the iodine pencils used for tattooing. He appreciates her eyes as instruments to outline her moral prohibitions on him. Her bans against whiskey, tobacco, bad language, lies, and color are less important to Parker than the rigor of submitting to a pattern of order, the very quality he sees in the performer's tattoos and feels lacking in his random body pictures.

Sarah Ruth's cutting speech serves as the electric tattooing implement. Her words strike with piercing exclamations. "'You don't talk no filth here!'" are her first clawing words. Once pinned, Parker accepts her stinging indictments, usually honed into scriptural shibboleths, until his rebellious body is riddled with warnings against the sins he enjoys. Sarah Ruth's last words cut him to the quick with the punishing stiletto of expulsion. The Byzantine Christ exceeds the allowance she makes for his habitual vices of lies and vanity. "'I don't want no idolator in this house!'" she cries. After she beats him senseless with the broom, her "eyes hardened still more" to prod her sentence into her stunned husband, now leaning against a pecan tree. O'Connor portrays a country female version of [Franz] Kafka's Commandant, who reigns in his story, "In the Penal Colony." Brandishing the broom as her scepter of control, Sarah Ruth runs a substation of Kafka's punitive province, where, as the officer in his story explains, guilt is never to be doubted. Sarah Ruth's Christian duty is to supervise the judicial rite of inscribing the suitable punishment into the body of the accused. The sinner must learn it on his body.

Gaining knowledge through flesh does not frighten Parker. However unfit he is for Sarah Ruth's home rule,

Parker's unconscious desire is for a total authority to which he can subject his mind. His initial thrill over the performer's tattoos is the feeling of integration between inner and outer order. The problem for Parker arises in the authorities to which he looks for meaning. He quits high school at sixteen, then quits trade school and works for six months at a garage to pay for tattoos. Revels of idle young manhood ensue; beer, women, and brawls sink Parker into a dissoluteness that incites his mother to drag him to a revival for correction. Parker naturally flees. He lies about his age to join the navy. In the navy he goes AWOL, is locked up in the brig, and is dishonorably discharged. Marriage follows, and Sarah Ruth becomes the last imposition of regimentation that fails to control Parker or to provide him with inner wholeness. The institutions are neither improbable choices nor inherently corrupt; they simply are inadequate for the man of wonder.

Only tattoos break Parker's cycle of discontent. The satisfaction from a new tattoo lasts no longer than a month, but for that time he feels excited. The high also creates in Parker a physiological dependency. After the contentment wears off, each tattoo exacerbates his sense of emptiness, and he craves another tattoo to alleviate his depression. Finally, all of his body except his back is tapestried. At first, static sentimentalities, such as the eagle perched on a cannon and his mother's name, do the trick. These inert images soon give way to drawings of dynamic pursuit in a panther and a tiger. Then the figures soar with hawks and lofty royal personages. Each tantalizes and betrays. As much as the progression in the designs indicates Parker's ascendent desire, the intensity exposes the impossibility of his ever finding satisfaction in lifeless pictures. He wants not the image but the actual stuff of wonder in himself. Without this vital feeling, his body remains a hodgepodge of disconnected pictures, lumpish sketches awaiting a power to bring them together as real. . . .

Defeat at the hands of Sarah Ruth, for whom Parker longs, denunciations and all, drives Parker to act in order to be recognized. Pregnancy no more softens her scorn for the sexual pleasure he needs than the marriage ceremony at the County Ordinary's office stops her incessant attacks, on Jesus' behalf, of Parker's profligacy. There is nothing left for him to do but to overcome his reluctance to decorate his back, which requires a mirror to admire, with a picture that would break through Sarah Ruth's prudery. A religious subject alone, he concludes, could seduce a wife whose love for God impugns love for her husband. At first, the idea of an opened Bible strikes Parker as a way to open Sarah Ruth's heart, but then he realizes that the tattoo would merely duplicate the real Bible that she already reads from: "He needed something better even than the Bible!". . .

In the fashion of reading a Hebrew text, Parker scans the tattoo artist's picture book from back to front for a suitable image of God. Reverse chronology takes him from modern sentimental representations through older daunting por-

---

THE SIGNIFICANCE OF THE TITLE "PARKER'S BACK"

In the following excerpt, Alice Hall Petry, professor of English at Southern Illinois University and the author of several critical studies on major American writers, examines the multiple meanings associated with the title "Parker's Back."

Although it may not be evident from a casual reading of the story, Christ himself gives Parker numerous signs that his next tattoo can be only on his back, literally 180° from his eyes—signs which sometimes seem like accidents, and other times seem like compulsive behavior; signs which generally somehow involve Sarah Ruth (the agent of his conversion, much as The Misfit is the agent of the grandmother's receptivity to Grace in "A Good Man Is Hard to Find"), and which always incorporate the key word "back." For example, the first time Sarah Ruth ever touched him, "Parker felt himself jolted *back* to life by her touch"; during his courtship of her, Parker "had no intention of taking any basket of peaches *back* [to her house] but the next day he found himself doing it"; when Sarah Ruth pushed him out of the truck to repulse his advances, he landed on his *back*; and her disapproval of Parker's working for a neighbor lady leads her to say, "You ought to go *back* to selling the fruits of the earth." Taken in isolation, of course, these and the many other references to the word "back" are not significant; but the unusually frequent occurrence of them in the story suggests that they form a message-laden pattern, a blatant sign from God that (a) the tattoo "had to be" on Parker's back and that, (b) paradoxically, Parker can move forward spiritually only by moving backwards physically. He can advance only through retreat, can face the future only by looking toward the past.

Alice Hall Petry, "O'Connor's 'Parker's Back'," *Explicator*, Winter 1988.

traits to the ordained one that commands in silent firmness that Parker "GO BACK" after passing it by. He flips the pages back to "the haloed head of a flat stern Byzantine Christ" awaiting him. The icon blares like an unveiling of itself and of Parker's inner need. Here, behind the feeble Christologies born of humanity's search for a pat on the back, there lies the one authority strong enough to compel Parker's obedience; and the face-to-face contact brings the hero out of himself. The will of God and the response of Parker are becoming one.

THE EYES OF THE BYZANTINE CHRIST

The source of power in this Christ is the eyes. Their "all-demanding" and "subtle power" seizes Parker from the printed page. Parker senses that the peculiar technique of the picture's little blocks creates the effect, and to preserve that force he insists that the artist stencil all the little blocks giving this Christ mysterious reality. The extraordinary pain of shouldering such stippled detail is not too high a price for Parker. To the artist's astonishment, Parker will pay with money and time and anguish to receive this riveting figure. Parker's demand that the tattooist copy the Christ exactly bespeaks an emotional consciousness of an aesthetic fact. The visual effect of a Byzantine mosaic derives from block lines. These mosaics are designed to be seen in the hazy light of lamps and candles. To heighten the light's play, the tiles are set in varying angles to create shimmering surfaces of movement akin to the intricate arabesque of brilliant colors on the performer's tattooed body that dazzles young Parker at the fair.

The eyes of the Byzantine Christ yanking Parker to life would be liquid and pale, like Parker's own slate-colored eyes—reflections of an unearthly realm far removed from the nearby alley and pool hall that Parker frequents when in the city. The mosaic composition in the hands of Byzantine artists works imaginatively around the piercing eyes. When the tattooist quits at midnight without completing the job, Parker feels cheated because the eyes are missing. The eyes complete the design, and they complete the work of the pursuer. After the Christ is finished, Parker looks into a mirror to see his back; he turns white and moves away from the reflection. The eyes in the mirrored face, however, continue to stare at Parker. Everything now rises to converge in these eyes. Not only do the eyes drive Parker to the eastern pole of Christendom, Byzantium, they absorb the disparate parts of Parker's tattooed body and marked soul into a harmonious unity. . . .

Like the horns of the bull in "Greenleaf," the sharp eyes embed in Parker the precedent for obedience that gives permanent meaning to the picture of Christ he freely chooses. O'Connor's use of the tattoo epitomizes her theology of matter. The Word made flesh communicates the Son's self-donation in service to the Father's plan for humankind. The divine Logos takes human form to pay for Adam's sin of disobedience by hanging on the cross. Christ's incarnation and crucifixion, His first and last acts, embrace the most thoroughgoing obedience to God's dictum. The Son's obedient death flows into the culminating event of the resurrection. The inauguration of universal judgment when humans are initiated into the divine reaffirms the dignity of flesh, as Christ's humanity becomes a permanent part of one world.

Without any notion or need of such theological commentary, Parker participates in God's promise of fulfillment. Parker is a simple man, obsessed by the necessity of getting a tattoo of God that will bring Sarah Ruth to heel and that will recapture joy. He wants rapture; and in reaching above and beyond himself, he learns that fullness must come from a greater-than-human source. However inarticulate, this awareness expresses a spiritual hope in O'Connor's world; and O'Connor makes use of whatever talent the character has to attain this possibility. With her sensualist, she will have to use his body to bring Parker to God. Since Christianity is a material religion in proclaiming that the Word is made flesh, O'Connor finds no impediment to showing how Parker's transcendence inheres in his body. Parker's yearning to feel the activity of God in his flesh confesses the basic Christian hope. Matter provides union with God. . . .

Before "Parker's Back" ends, God gives the hero an intimate experience of the great cost as well as the privilege of bearing the sacred face to the heathens. After the fight, Parker speeds home to Sarah Ruth, who, he believes, understands God and will comfort him in the confusion created by the tattoo. Befuddled as ever in seeking consolation for his spiritual anxiety in the sexual, Parker nevertheless feels a newness in and around himself. The familiar surroundings of the ride home seem to be part of "a new country." The dawn rises like an ally. Several yellow streaks flicker as he pounds on the door to be admitted to his house. Suddenly, a tree blazes with the light from the morning sun; the bright ally declares himself. Again, the ally rises to prod Parker into battle by reminding him of the all-demanding will that controls him. A long shaft of light nails him against the locked door, and the pain promised by this lance of light comes in the form of Sarah Ruth. Her cold unfeeling voice, insisting that Parker identify himself, pins the hero to the truth about himself that he has buried beneath twenty-eight years of denial. He whispers the watchword, his names, "'Obadiah Elihue!'"

Obadiah means "servant of God." The title designates how Parker must conduct himself in the new country that he has entered. Performing duties to the absolute will lead to the rapture he seeks. After he murmurs his first name, light pours through his body as a promise of joy. The entangled web of his soul, imprinted with his disconnected tattoos, fuses into an arabesque of creation—"a garden of trees and birds and beasts." Parker's body, like the colorful hallelujah parade concluding "Revelation," presents a version of the peacock's splendor displayed. Having become a paradise of wonder, Obadiah freely gives his second name, Elihue, which affirms the God he serves. *Elihue* means "my God is he." With the initials O.E. acquiring substance, Parker's flesh is now made word. He feels himself to be the visible dwelling of glory.

CHRONOLOGY

1925

Mary Flannery O'Connor born to Edward Francis and Regina Cline O'Connor on March 25 in Savannah, Georgia. F. Scott Fitzgerald publishes *The Great Gatsby.*

1929

William Faulkner publishes *The Sound and the Fury.*

1929–37

Following the stock market crash of October 29, 1929, the country enters the Great Depression.

1933

The Eighteenth Amendment, which prohibits the sale and consumption of alcoholic beverages, is repealed. President Roosevelt introduces the "New Deal," his plan to end the depression.

LATE 1930s

Mr. O'Connor develops disseminated lupus; family moves to Milledgeville, Georgia, the home of the Cline family since before the Civil War.

1939

John Steinbeck publishes *The Grapes of Wrath.*

1939–45

World War II.

1941

Mr. O'Connor dies of lupus. The U.S. enters World War II after the Japanese attack Pearl Harbor.

1945

Mary Flannery graduates from Georgia State College for Women. Japan surrenders after the U.S. drops atomic bombs on Hiroshima and Nagasaki; World War II ends. Harry Truman becomes president (1945–53).

1945–47

Attends Writers Workshop at State University of Iowa; drops "Mary" from her name.

1946

"The Geranium" published in *Accent.*

1947

Earns M.F.A. degree. Begins her first novel, *Wise Blood.*

1947–48

Lives at Yaddo writer's colony in Sarasota Springs, New York.

1949

Lives in New York City. Chapters from her first novel, *Wise Blood*, published in *Partisan Review.* Leaves NYC to live with friends Sally and Robert Fitzgerald in Connecticut.

1950

Suffers first attack of lupus in December and returns to Georgia.

1950–53

Korean War. U.S. senator McCarthy holds hearings accusing politicians and other public figures of being Communists. (In 1954 he is condemned for his activities by the U.S. Senate.)

1951

Moves with mother to dairy farm, "Andalusia," five miles from Milledgeville. J.D. Salinger publishes *The Catcher in the Rye.*

1952

Wise Blood published. Ernest Hemingway publishes *The Old Man and the Sea;* Ralph Ellison publishes *Invisible Man.*

1953

Awarded Kenyon Fellowship. "A Good Man Is Hard to Find" published in *Modern Writing I.* Dwight D. Eisenhower becomes president (1953–61).

1954

"The Life You Save May Be Your Own" awarded second prize in the O. Henry awards for short stories. The U.S. Supreme Court declares segregation in public schools to be unconstitutional.

1955

First collection of short stories, *A Good Man Is Hard to Find and Other Stories*, published. "A Circle in the Fire" wins second prize in the O. Henry awards. O'Connor begins to use crutches as a result of her declining health.

1957

"Greenleaf" wins first prize in the O. Henry awards. O'Connor receives National Institute of Arts and Letters grant.

1958

Travels with her mother to Lourdes and Rome. Audience with the Pope.

1959

Receives Ford Foundation grant.

1960

Her second novel, *The Violent Bear It Away*, published. John F. Kennedy is elected president; O'Connor is a Kennedy supporter. Seventy thousand blacks and whites participate in sit-ins to desegregate public facilities.

1960–61

The U.S. military becomes increasingly involved in the Vietnam conflict.

1963

Receives an honorary degree from Smith College. "Everything That Rises Must Converge" awarded first prize in the O. Henry awards. John F. Kennedy is assassinated; Lyndon B. Johnson becomes president.

1964

Dies on August 3 at Milledgeville Hospital. "Revelation" wins first prize in the O. Henry awards.

1965

Everything That Rises Must Converge published.

1969

Mystery and Manners, an edited selection of prose drawn from her lectures and essays, published.

1971

The Complete Stories of Flannery O'Connor, which contains

all of her previously published stories, her early stories submitted in fulfillment of her M.F.A. degree, and early versions
of both novels, published.

1972

The Complete Stories of Flannery O'Connor awarded National
Book Award.

FOR FURTHER RESEARCH

WORKS BY FLANNERY O'CONNOR

Wise Blood (1952)
A Good Man Is Hard to Find and Other Stories (1955)
The Violent Bear It Away (1960)
Everything That Rises Must Converge (1965)
Mystery and Manners: Occasional Prose (1969)
The Complete Stories of Flannery O'Connor (1971)
The Habit of Being: Letters of Flannery O'Connor (1979)

BIOGRAPHIES

Robert Coles, *Flannery O'Connor's South.* Baton Rouge: Louisiana State University Press, 1980.

Lorine M. Getz, *Flannery O'Connor: Her Life, Library, and Book Reviews.* New York: The Edwin Mellen Press, 1980.

Richard Giannone, *Flannery O'Connor, Hermit Novelist.* Urbana: University of Illinois Press, 2000.

Rosemary Magee, *Conversations with Flannery O'Connor.* Jackson: University Press of Mississippi, 1987.

Barbara McKenzie, *Flannery O'Connor's Georgia.* Athens: University of Georgia Press, 1980.

LITERARY CRITICISM

Frederick Asals, *Flannery O'Connor: The Imagination of Extremity.* Athens: University of Georgia Press, 1982.

Jon Lance Bacon, *Flannery O'Connor and Cold War Culture.* Cambridge, England: Cambridge University Press, 1993.

Susan Balee, *Flannery O'Connor: Literary Prophet of the South.* New York: Chelsea House Publishers, 1994.

Jill Pelaez Baumgaertner, *Flannery O'Connor: A Proper Scaring.* Chicago: Cornerstone, 1998.

Harold Bloom, ed., *Modern Critical Views: Flannery O'Connor.* New York: Chelsea House Publishers, 1986.

Robert H. Brinkmeyer Jr., *The Art & Vision of Flannery O'Connor.* Baton Rouge: Louisiana State University Press, 1989.

Preston M. Browning Jr., *Flannery O'Connor.* Carbondale: Southern Illinois University Press, 1974.

John Desmond, *Risen Sons: Flannery O'Connor's Vision of History.* Athens: University of Georgia Press, 1987.

Leon V. Driskell and Joan T. Brittain, *The Eternal Crossroads: The Art of Flannery O'Connor.* Lexington: The University Press of Kentucky, 1971.

Kathleen Feeley, *Flannery O'Connor: Voice of the Peacock.* New Brunswick, NJ: Rutgers University Press, 1972.

Melvin J. Friedman and Beverly Lyon Clark, eds., *Critical Essays on Flannery O'Connor.* Boston: G.K. Hall, 1985.

Melvin J. Friedman and Lewis A. Lawson, eds., *The Added Dimension: The Art and Mind of Flannery O'Connor.* New York: Fordham University Press, 1977.

Marshal Bruce Gentry, *Flannery O'Connor's Religion of the Grotesque.* Jackson: University Press of Mississippi, 1986.

Lorine M. Getz, *Nature and Grace in Flannery O'Connor's Fiction.* New York: The Edwin Mellen Press, 1982.

Richard Giannone, *Flannery O'Connor and the Mystery of Love.* Urbana: University of Illinois Press, 1989.

James A. Grimshaw Jr., *The Flannery O'Connor Companion.* Westport, CT: Greenwood Press, 1981.

Josephine Hendin, *The World of Flannery O'Connor.* Bloomington: Indiana University Press, 1970.

Stanley Edgar Hyman, *Flannery O'Connor.* Minneapolis: University of Minnesota Press, 1966.

Edward Kessler, *Flannery O'Connor and the Language of Apocalypse.* Princeton, NJ: Princeton University Press, 1986.

Carter W. Martin, *The True Country: Themes in the Fiction of Flannery O'Connor.* Nashville, TN: The Vanderbilt University Press, 1968.

John R. May, *The Pruning Word: The Parables of Flannery O'Connor.* Notre Dame, IN: University of Notre Dame Press, 1976.

Dorothy Tuck McFarland, *Flannery O'Connor.* New York: Frederick Ungar, 1976.

Joanne Halleran McMullen, *Writing Against God: Language as Message in the Literature of Flannery O'Connor.* Macon, GA: Mercer University Press, 1996.

Gilbert H. Muller, *Nightmares and Visions: Flannery O'Connor and the Catholic Grotesque.* Athens: University of Georgia Press, 1972.

Miles Orvell, *Invisible Parade: The Fiction of Flannery O'Connor.* Philadelphia: Temple University Press, 1972.

Brian Abel Ragen, *A Wreck on the Road to Damascus: Innocence, Guilt, and Conversion in Flannery O'Connor.* Chicago: Loyola University Press, 1989.

Sura P. Rath and Mary Neff Shaw, eds., *Flannery O'Connor: New Perspectives.* Athens: University of Georgia Press, 1996.

Carol Schloss, *Flannery O'Connor's Dark Comedies: The Limits of Inference.* Baton Rouge: Lousiana State University Press, 1980.

Martha Stevens, *The Question of Flannery O'Connor.* Baton Rouge: Louisiana State University Press, 1973.

Margaret Early Whitt, *Understanding Flannery O'Connor.* Columbia: University of South Carolina Press, 1995.

INDEX